LMS-LM REGION

Above:
Rebuilt 'Royal Scot' No 46120 *Royal Inniskilling Fusilier* pulls away from the booked stop at Lichfield with the 15.45 Euston-Manchester on 19 July 1952. *T. Lakin*

Overleaf:
APT-P unit 370.003 at Euston on 11 February 1980 contrasts with the more homely outlines of an '86/2' on the adjacent track. *R. L. Sewell*

86 247
370 003

1

PASSENGER TRAIN FORMATIONS 1923-1983

LMS-LM REGION

CLIVE S. CARTER

LONDON

IAN ALLAN LTD

Contents

Front cover:
The 'Royal Scot' at Oxenholme in August 1933, hauled by 'Royal Scot' class 4-6-0 No 6158 *The Loyal Regiment*.
From a painting by George Heiron

Back cover, top:
Locomotive-hauled Pullman cars replaced the 'Blue Pullman' sets when the Euston electrification was completed. No 86 226 heads the up 'Manchester Pullman' at Ardwick on 10 August 1978. *G. S. Cutts*

Back cover, bottom:
The 11.20 Birmingham-Glasgow leaving Preston in September 1954. Essentially the whole train was formed of BR standard stock by this time. Only the Period 3 Restaurant First, the third vehicle behind the loco, and a Corridor Third near the rear were of LMS origin. Class 2P 4-4-0 No 40656 pilots rebuilt 'Royal Scot' 4-6-0 No 46138 *The London Irish Rifleman*. *W. S. Garth*

First published 1987

ISBN 0 7110 1606 2

Published by Ian Allan Ltd, Shepperton, Surrey; and printed by Ian Allan Printing Ltd at their works at Coombelands in Runnymede, England

Introduction

Most writers have discussed the locomotive at the head of a passenger train, with little regard for the coaches behind. This book aims to reverse the situation and focuses on the arrangement of coaches behind the locomotive — ie the train formation. Its purpose is to present the formation of selected LMS trains, and their BR successors, between 1923 and 1983. Attention is concentrated primarily on express trains, but cross-country and local trains are also included. Where available information permits, the specific types of coaches employed are noted.

A selection of the day and night expresses which left the London termini for the North is presented. Selections have also been made to encompass a wide geographical area of the railway network. Some named trains are included but no attempt has been made to cover them all. Consideration is also given to inter-company workings and to trains which contained uncommon coaching stock.

A description of all the changes in formation which occurred for any long-lived train can become rather extensive. A study of the 'Midday Scot' published in *Railway World* (June and July 1985) required 11 pages just to describe the 1923-39 period. If this was followed here, only about a dozen trains could be addressed. Some constraints have therefore been applied to the train formations described here; only the summer timetable is considered; formations are given at approximately 10-year intervals; significant changes in the intervening periods are indicated when available information permits; attention is mainly concentrated on the down direction; in many cases the up train was simply the balancing working but in some instances there were major differences, particularly when the down train divided en route. Saturday formations are omitted; many of the weekday sets were strengthened or modified on a Saturday and it is considered that this additional degree of complexity is best avoided.

The information presented in this book has been obtained from official sources. Each company, and later Region, published a series of pamphlets describing the formation of every train. They were called 'Passenger Train Marshalling' books by the LMS and this description remains in general use on BR today. The period of applicability usually corresponded with that of the working timetable but the LMS published three series of books per year in May, July and September. Individual Marshalling books are prepared for the Western, Midland, Central and Scottish Divisions. Suburban and local workings were dealt with separately. The format of the carriage working books has changed very little during this century. After nationalisation, the contents remained much the same, although a universal rolling stock code system, based on that used by the LNER, was introduced. The 1984 LM Region book closely resembles that published by the LNWR 70 years earlier, and the LMS book of 50 years ago.

In addition to showing the formation for each train the balancing working was shown. The total seating capacity and weight of the train were given, as was the number of seats for each coach. As discussed later, some seating arrangements were unique to certain coach types, thus aiding in their identification here.

It has been possible to identify the type of restaurant car used in most sets. Concurrent with the Marshalling book, the LMS (and later LM Region) published a separate pamphlet titled *Breakfast, Luncheon, Tea and Dining Car*

Circuits which specified the class and seating for each restaurant car circuit. Most types were self-evident from the data given. Some pre-grouping cars, however, had identical seating to the LMS-built cars and it was not always possible to determine which was employed. The circuit book, however, did specifically require a 'new pattern vehicle' for some sets. The specified seating has also provided an indication of the type of vehicle.

A brief survey of coaching stock is presented first. This reviews the coaching stock which went to form the LMS fleet in 1923. Vehicles subsequently built by the company, and by British Railways are also considered. A list of coach drawing references are included.

Top:
'Jubilee' 4-6-0 No 45562 *Alberta* emerges from Blea Moor Tunnel with the 6.40 Birmingham-Glasgow (via Leeds) on 26 August 1967.
M. S. Welch

Above:
A Swindon 6-car 'Trans-Pennine' DMU leaves Manchester Victoria on 22 September 1976 with the 09.44 Hull-Liverpool. *Brian Morrison*

LMS Coaching Stock

The London Midland and Scottish Railway had almost 27,000 passenger-rated vehicles when it was formed in 1923. The majority came from the London & North Western, Midland, Caledonian and Glasgow & South Western Railways. Several other railway companies went into the formation of the LMS but their combined contribution was only 7%. A summary is given below:

Company	*Uniform Class*	*Composite*	*Other Stock*	*Miscellaneous*		*Total*
CR	1,765	525	710	Restaurant Car	12	3,040
				Sleeping Car	13	
				PO Van	15	
FR	—	—	—			361
G&SWR	1,072	103	413	Restaurant Car	8	1,604
				PO Van	8	
HR	203	92	483	Sleeping Car	2	789
				PO Van	9	
LNWR*	7,422	2,679	3,843	Restaurant Car	103	14,176
				Sleeping Car	49	
				Electric Motor Coaches	223	
				Trailer Coaches	290	
				Steam Rail Motor Cars	24	
				PO Van	60	
MR	3,141	1,005	1,771	Restaurant Car	80	6,019
				Sleeping Car	22	
				Electric Motor Car	48	
				Trailer Car	49	
				Electric Motor Vehicle**	20	
MCR						71
NSR	267	74	193			534
S&MJR	7	10	11			28
WR	56	14	1			71
					Total	26,693

*The L&YR stock taken over by the LNWR in 1922 was:

L&YR	2,976	751	579	Restaurant Car	4	4,310
				Electric Motor Car	119	
				Trailer Car	122	

**Burton and Ashby Light Railway

Data from *Railway Yearbook, 1923*

The London & North Western Railway had by far the largest fleet of passenger vehicles of the companies which formed the LMS. Having taken over the Lancashire & Yorkshire Railway in 1922 it was able to supply more than 14,000 vehicles to the new company. The development of the fleet is described in *An Illustrated History of LNWR Coaches* by David Jenkinson (Oxford Publishing Company). He showed that the coach styles produced at different periods could be characterised primarily by the type of roof. The total number of vehicles built are summarised in this way below:

	Arc Roof (1893-1903)	*Cove Roof (1903-1907)*	*Elliptical Roof (1907-1923)*
Corridor Coaches	762	154	1,121
Non-Corridor Coaches	2,569	412	799

Several different body lengths were incorporated in the totals. Essentially all these coaches were taken over by the LMS. Restaurant and Sleeping Cars built before 1907 had clerestory roofs, an elliptical style being adopted thereafter.

The takeover of the Lancashire & Yorkshire Railway by the LNWR in 1922 added about 3,700 passenger coaches to the 'Premier Line's' stock. About a quarter of them were six-wheel vehicles, but the remainder were bogie stock. Over 1,000 were 49ft-long, arc roof, non-corridor bogie coaches built in a 10-year period from 1894. An elliptical roof was used for later non-corridor coaches. Around 150 corridor coaches had gangways. Most of them were 56ft long and by 1909 an elliptical roof was standard. A number of gangwayed open coaches were also built. A review of the coaches has recently been published — namely *Lancashire and Yorkshire Passenger Stock* by R. W. Rush (Oakwood Press).

The next largest fleet came from the Midland Railway. The coaching stock owned by this company has been recently reviewed by Messrs Jenkinson and Essery in *Midland Carriages* (Oxford Publishing Company), and by Lacy and Dow in *Midland Railway Carriages* (Wild Swan Publications). Jenkinson and Essery show that the gangwayed corridor stock consisted of 854 coaches (including restaurant and sleeping cars), almost all of which were clerestory roofed apart from 91 elliptical roof vehicles. The majority had a body length of 54ft. A second category, identified as non-corridor express stock, contained 862 coaches including 65 six-wheel vehicles. Two-thirds of this total were of clerestory roof style with the remainder being arc or elliptical roof types. A total of 3,605 non-corridor 'ordinary' coaches were identified. Nearly half were non-bogie vehicles and about 80% had arc roofs.

The next largest contribution came from the Caledonian Railway which provided about 2,300 coaches for the LMS. Bogie stock was introduced in 1886 but it was not until 1889 that the construction of a standard series of 45ft non-corridor coaches commenced. Several hundred of these went into service during the following 10 years. The most famous Caledonian corridor coaches were the 'Grampian' vehicles. Construction commenced in 1903, and seven different types were built. These 65ft-long, gangwayed, corridor coaches were carried on six-wheel bogies and had a slightly flattened elliptical roof. From 1912 the Caledonian adopted a standard length of 57ft for both corridor and non-corridor stock. Restaurant Cars were never built by the Caledonian. Second-hand cars purchased from the West Coast Joint Stock were initially used. Starting in 1914, Pullman cars were employed for catering. A total of 15 Pullmans had been delivered at the time of grouping.

In the case of the G&SWR, just over 1,000 coaches were available at grouping. Bogie stock was introduced in 1893 and a number of 43ft-long non-corridor coaches were built. However, six-wheel stock was also continued for some time. Corridor stock did not appear until 1899, when a complete train was built for the Glasgow-Stranraer service. A series of non-corridor vehicles built in 1907 were about 70ft long. They had elliptical roofs and were carried on six-wheel bogies. Some of the final developments of G&SWR carriage design included 57ft gangwayed corridor stock for the Glasgow-Carlisle services.

Almost two-thirds of the Highland Railway passenger carrying stock was made up of four-wheel and six-wheel coaches. However, over 100 bogie coaches had been constructed since the mid-1890s, 26 being fitted with gangways, these being almost equally divided between composites and thirds. Two Sleeping Cars were built to work between Inverness and Glasgow but they were not gangwayed. The Highland constructed several different types of PO Van including four-wheel, six-wheel and bogie versions. A description of the stock is given in *Carriages and Wagons of the Highland Railway* by D. L. G. Hunter (Turntable Enterprises).

Only the total number of passenger vehicles of the Furness Railway was recorded in the *Railway Yearbook* as tabulated above. Fortunately R. W. Rush in his book *The Furness Railway* (Oakwood Press) has provided a good summary. In 1923 there were 144 six-wheel coaches. Bogie stock appeared in 1897 and small batches were built at irregular intervals until 1921. Gangwayed corridor stock was first constructed in 1904 but only 14 coaches were built during the next 20 years. The last six built exceeded 60ft in length.

Although not a large company, the North Staffordshire Railway had quite a few bogie vehicles. Early versions had an arc roof but this was changed to elliptical in 1909. Body length was about 49ft and the Composites had a semi-corridor interior. The Maryport & Carlisle Railway primarily used six-wheel coaches for its passenger services. It was not devoid of bogie stock, however, owning a few bogie composites. The Stratford Upon Avon & Midland Junction Railway and the Wirral Railway provided a combined total of 99 vehicles.

The West Coast Joint Stock (WCJS) which worked the Anglo-Scottish trains was jointly owned by the London & North Western Railway, which had about a two-thirds share, and by the Caledonian Railway which held the remainder. At grouping, the passenger stock totalled 675 vehicles. They are incorporated into the totals shown above for the two owning companies, being divided according to the percentage of ownership. All coach construction was at Wolverton (LNWR) but there were often differences between contemporary LNWR and WCJS vehicles. The types of roof noted above for LNWR coaches also applied to those of the WCJS except that the cove roof was not used. Details of the vehicles can be found in Jenkinson's book on the LNWR, and in *A Register of West Coast Joint Stock* by R. M. Casserly and P. A. Millard (Historical Model Railway Society). The Midland Railway also owned joint stock with the G&SWR and with the North British Railway for services to Glasgow and Edinburgh respectively. The vehicles were built by the Midland but the quantities were much smaller than in the case of the WCJS. Information can be found in the books on the Midland Railway referred to above.

The history of the LMS coaches has been described in detail in *LMS Coaches* by D. Jenkinson and R. J. Essery (Oxford Publishing Company). These authors identified three main categories of coach style which could be identified with the period in which they were built. They were denoted as Periods 1-3 and this convention has been adopted throughout this book. The corridor stock is briefly reviewed below. It should be emphasised that there was overlapping between each period; only the key features of each are noted.

Period 1 (1923-1928/9)

Most of the Period 1 coaches had a high-waisted, wood-panelled, fully-beaded body. The roof was elliptical and each compartment had an exterior door. There was a strong Midland influence on the designs. This was particularly apparent in the open stock, which had a twin window arrangement in each seating bay.

Period 2 (1929-1932)

A new low-waisted style was adopted. Compartment doors were eliminated, and a large, square-cornered glass window was provided for each compartment. Glass vane ventilators were fitted over these windows. Initially wood-panelled and beaded bodies were continued, but the designs were gradually changed over to steel panels.

Period 3 (1933 Onwards)

Flush steel-panelled bodies, rounded window corners and a ribbed roof were characteristic of this period. Sliding ventilators were incorporated in the windows. The style of stock has often been referred to as 'Stanier'. Coaches produced after nationalisation had a circular toilet window and were known as 'Porthole' stock.

The standard body length of the LMS coach was 57ft. Longer vehicles were produced but these were mainly Restaurant Cars and Sleeping Cars. The longest were 69ft Sleeping Cars built during Period 3. There were some shorter types, including Kitchen Cars and most Full Brakes.

Unfortunately, the LMS numbering system did not give any indication of the area to which the coach was allocated. Open stock was turned out in large numbers during Periods 1 and 2. Just over half of the Period 1 style coaches were of this type. While open stock production continued during Period 3, with several hundred vehicles built, greater emphasis was placed on compartment stock. Only a few Restaurant Cars appeared during Period 2 and no Sleeping Cars were built in this style. Most of the Kitchen Cars were constructed in Period 1 and quite a few Sleeping Cars also emerged during this period.

A summary of LMS Gangwayed Coaches

	Period 1	*Period 2*	*Period 3*
Corr First	23	—	86
Corr Brake First	25	25	27
Corr Third	290	10	1,442
Corr Brake Third	147	100	1,363
Corr Composite	246	48	1,027
Corr Composite Brake	134	70	75
Open First	66	25	107
Semi-Open First	5	11	—
Open Brake First Lounge	5	—	—
Open Third	846	376	939
Open Restaurant Third	60	25	9
Open Brake Third	95	—	167
Open Composite	20	—	39
Kitchen Car	73	—	35
Restaurant First	—	24	20
Restaurant Third	—	—	44
Restaurant Composite	6	12	13
Sleeper First	43*	—	51
Sleeper Composite	12*	—	13
Sleeper Third	85	—	40

*Includes vehicles with LNWR styling

The Carriage Marshalling books specified the seating requirements (or length) for each coach in the formation. Since certain seating arrangements were unique to a period, it is possible in these instances to determine the style of coach allocated to the train.

Some of the main features of all three period styles discussed above were also applicable to non-corridor stock. Body length was mainly 57ft for general service stock but some sets for specific services were made up of 54ft vehicles. Push-pull fitted coaches were also built from non-corridor stock.

Right:
LMS Period 2 Semi-Open First. *BR*

Right:
LMS Period 2 Open Third. *BR*

Right:
Period 2 Open Brake Third. *BR*

BR Coaching Stock

Coaching stock continued to be built to LMS designs during the first five years after nationalisation. In 1950 the first BR standard coaches (later known as Mk 1) appeared. The standard body length adopted for gangwayed stock was 63ft 6in. Sufficient different types, including catering vehicles, had been built in enough quantities that it was possible in the following year to form complete sets of the new stock for several named trains, of which two are discussed later. Production of the new vehicles by BR workshops and contractors continued at a rapid pace. By the mid-1950s many of the front line, and some secondary, train sets were either entirely asembled from these coaches or at least contained a significant proportion. Sleeping Cars were produced in volume during the latter half of the 1950s, and large numbers of restaurant cars followed. Construction of Mk 1 passenger coaches ceased in 1964. A detailed review of the history and development of this stock has been conducted by Keith Parkin and published by the Historical Model Railway Society as *Locomotive Hauled Mark 1 Coaching Stock of British Railways*. In view of the fact that little information is readily available on the allocation of the Mk 1 coaches for the first years of their existence, this is shown in the following table for 1957:

Type	*London Midland*	*Scottish*
RFO	4-6	
RTO	1003-5	
FO	3000/1/2/8-47	3007
TO	3700-72, 3947-69, 4358-72, 4422-42, 4475-87	3987-97, 4244-57
FK	13004-29/60-4/85-97, 13108-10/75-88, 13220/1	13055-9/81-4
CK	15001-20/50-2, 15181-270, 15311-42/50-97, 15433-6/53/4, 15626-83, 15821-60, 15916-16006	15146-80, 15346-9, 15418-24, 15523-32, 14543-62
BCK	21025-32	21017-9, 21112-7
TK	24000-24149, 24397-24446/57-68, 24576-90, 24676-90, 24819-24918, 25283-330, 25455-7	24170-9, 24240-301, 24394-6, 24557-68, 24651-75, 24721-45/92-5, 24816-8, 24919-43
BTK	34000-6/11-148, 34285-9, 34358-71, 34389-99, 34451-70, 34501-84, 34655-724, 35040-116	34188-224, 34316-25, 34400-12/31-50
RK	80004-6	

Notes:
1 Regional prefix (M or SC) to number omitted above.
2 Prototype vehicles excluded.

The first batch of Mk 2 coaches, which were Corridor Firsts, was produced in 1963/64. After an interval of two years new stock was built for the Euston electrification programme, and by the end of 1966 a total of 322 Mk 2 coaches, over half of which were Open Seconds, had been built. Following the decision of the BRB to change over to air braking the next vehicles (Mk 2a) were fitted accordingly, but they went to the East Coast in 1967/68. They were followed by a change in body style, Mk 2b coaches having 3ft-wide entrance doorways and wrap-around ends. The Mk 2c coaches, were designed to be fitted with air conditioning although this was not done. A major advancement took place in 1970 when the Mk 2d version was built. It was fully air conditioned and was externally recognisable by narrow tinted windows devoid of ventilators. The Mk 2e, which only went to the London Midland Region, had slightly smaller lavatories, to allow the Open Second capacity to be increased to 64 seats (there had only been 62 seats since the change of body style from Mk 2b). The final development was the Mk 2f in 1973, which had a modified interior and improved seating. A detailed review of the development of the Mk 2 coach fleet was given in the June 1971 *Railway World*.

The Mk 3 coach was introduced in 1972. The body was 75ft 5in long and the same body shell was used for First and Second Class vehicles. Vehicles were delivered to the LM Region and into the IC125 sets. Later Mk 3 developments included the construction of 28 Restaurant Buffet Cars, and a fleet of InterCity Sleepers to replace the Mk 1 types.

Non-corridor standard stock was also built. There were several types including open types for dense suburban routes. The standard body length was 56ft 11in but a 63ft 5in-long version was also built for the Southern and Western Regions. Vehicle allocation, at the beginning of 1962, to the regions covered in this book is shown below:

	London Midland	*Scottish*
Composite	15	27
Composite — Lavatory	—	—
Brake Second	86	63
Second	28	44
Open Second — Lavatory	—	—
Open Second	8	—

Above:
BR Mk 1 Corridor Composite. *BR*

Main Line Formations

The formations of selected trains are presented in the following pages. Trains leaving London are given first in departure time order. Those from other departure points follow in alphabetical order. The formations are given for the summer timetable. Saturday workings are excluded. **The vehicle nearest the left-hand margin in the schematic diagrams and at the top of each formation listing is the leading vehicle of the train (ie attached to the locomotive).**

Each formation is itemised in two complementary forms. The first is a horizontal schematic diagram in which each vehicle is represented by a boxed, two-character letter code, which is intended to provide the reader with a brief 'at a glance' indication of the basic marshalling of the train. The second, which is set immediately below the diagram, is a textual listing of the stock with details, where appropriate, of vehicle length, seating capacity, origin of design and exceptional working. Alongside, the points of original departure and final destination of specific vehicles is given where either or both differ from those of the main formation.

The LMS (and LM Region) usually specified the number of seats for each coach. This convention has been followed here. Seating in BR standard stock is not quoted as such information is readily available. (See *Rolling Stock Recognition 1: Coaching Stock* by C. J. Marsden and *ABC BR Hauled Coaching Stock* — both published by Ian Allan Ltd.) The only exceptions shown are for the BR Open Seconds which were built with 48 seats, rather than the normal 64, and the Restaurant Cars of which there are several different kinds.

Unless otherwise indicated, the formation entirely consists of stock owned by the operating company appropriate to the time period shown. Where the formation is principally made up from one owner's stock, this is listed below the formation, deviations being noted against the appropriate vehicle. Where the stock varies throughout the formation, the original owner of each coach is shown.

Vehicles fitted with seats and a kitchen are referred to as Restaurant Cars here. When 'Open' is included (ie Restaurant Open First) this indicates a car externally lettered as a Restaurant Car but without a kitchen. The term 'Restaurant (Car)' has been used throughout, since this was adopted by BR; the LMS called them 'Dining Cars' in prewar days. Open stock was referred to as 'vestibuled' by the LMS; 'Open' is used here following BR practice.

While the balancing train departure time is given, it should be emphasised that its formation could be different to that shown. Some sets were split after arrival, or different vehicles attached during the balancing return. Space considerations preclude a detailed review.

Extracts of some of the general notes regarding formations given in the Carriage Marshalling books are quoted in Appendix A.

Key to Schematic Train Formation Diagrams

The formations shown are for the maximum extent of the train and includes vehicles used only on specific weekdays, readers are advised to refer to the actual listings for details.

Hauled Passenger Stock

B Non-Corridor Brake Third
B1 Brake First
B2 Brake Second
B3 Brake Third
BC Brake Composite
BU (Miniature) Buffet
BV Brake Van

C Non-Corridor Composite
C1 Corridor First
C2 Corridor Second
C3 Corridor Third
CA Cafeteria Car
CC Corridor Composite

KB Kitchen Buffet
KC Kitchen Car

N1 Non-Corridor First

O1 Open First
O2 Open Second
O3 Open Third
OB Observation Car
OC Open Composite

PB Pullman/Parlour Brake
PC Pullman/Parlour Car
PK Pullman/Parlour Kitchen

R1 Restaurant First
R2 Restaurant Second
R3 Restaurant Third
RB Restaurant/Buffet
RC Restaurant Composite
RU Restaurant Unclassified

SA Saloon
S1 Sleeper First
S2 Sleeper Second
S3 Sleeper Third
SC Sleeper Composite
SE Sleeper Either Class
SP Sleeper Either Class (Pantry)

T3 Tea Car Third

UN Unknown

Hauled NPCCS Stock

MV Milk Van
PS Post Office Sorting Van
PV Post Office Van
SV Scenery Van
UV Utility/Parcels Van

'Blue Pullman' Stock

MB Motor Brake First
MK Motor Kitchen First
TP Trailer Parlour First

Diesel Multiple-Unit Stock

Mb Motor Brake Second
M2 Motor Second
TB Trailer Buffet

Right:
Stanier 'Black Five' 4-6-0 No 44686, fitted with double chimney and Caprotti valve gear passes Prestatyn on 8 August 1962 with a Manchester-Holyhead train including both 'Porthole' and BR Mk 1 stock.
Derek Cross

Abbreviations used in Train Formation Listings:

Some categories of information relevant to certain vehicles are expressed in abbreviated form and follow the vehicle description as outlined below.

Seating Capacity

This is expressed as a bracketed number, ie **Corr Third (42)**. In the case of Composite stock the first figure is the number of First Class seats, ie **Corr Composite (18/24)**.

Vehicle Length

This is expressed in feet, ie **Open Third 60ft**.

Original Ownership

Where a variety of vehicle types is included in one formation, the following abbreviations may appear:

(BR1)—BR Mk 1 stock
(GWR)—GWR-designed vehicle
(LMS)—LMS-designed vehicle
(LNER)—LNER-designed vehicle
(M&NB)—Midland & North British stock
(WCJS)—West Coast Joint stock

Exceptional Working

In many cases, certain vehicles were only included in a formation on specific days of the week. Such cases are expressed as follows: **(MO)** Mondays only; **(TO)** Tuesdays only; **(WO)** Wednesdays only; **(ThO)** Thursdays only; **(FO)** Fridays only. Combinations of these may also apply, ie **(MThO)** Mondays and Thursdays only.

Train Marshalling

In many cases, the listed formations include vehicles which have a different point of departure and/or destination to the main formation — the vehicles concerned being attached or detached at appropriate locations en route. Such information is set alongside the vehicle(s) concerned and is best illustrated by the following examples:

Different Point of Departure
Open Third 60ft — (*ex*-Liverpool)

Different Destination
Corr Composite (18/24) — Dundee

Different Point of Departure and Destination
Corr Brake Composite (GWR) Plymouth-Glasgow

Summary

The various abbreviations and notes outlined above will often be found in combination. To finally illustrate the simplicity of the system, the following fictitious example is offered:

Open Composite (18/18) 60ft (LM) (ThO)
— Leeds-Morecambe

This represents a 60ft LMS vehicle with 18 First and 18 Third Class seats, running in the Leeds-Morecambe portion of the train on Thursdays only.

Right:
A Glasgow-Stranraer train at Ayr, probably in the late 1920s. The leading vehicles, including the Pullman car, only worked between Glasgow and Ayr (or Girvan). The train is headed by ex-Glasgow & South Western 4-4-0 No 14509.
W. Rear collection

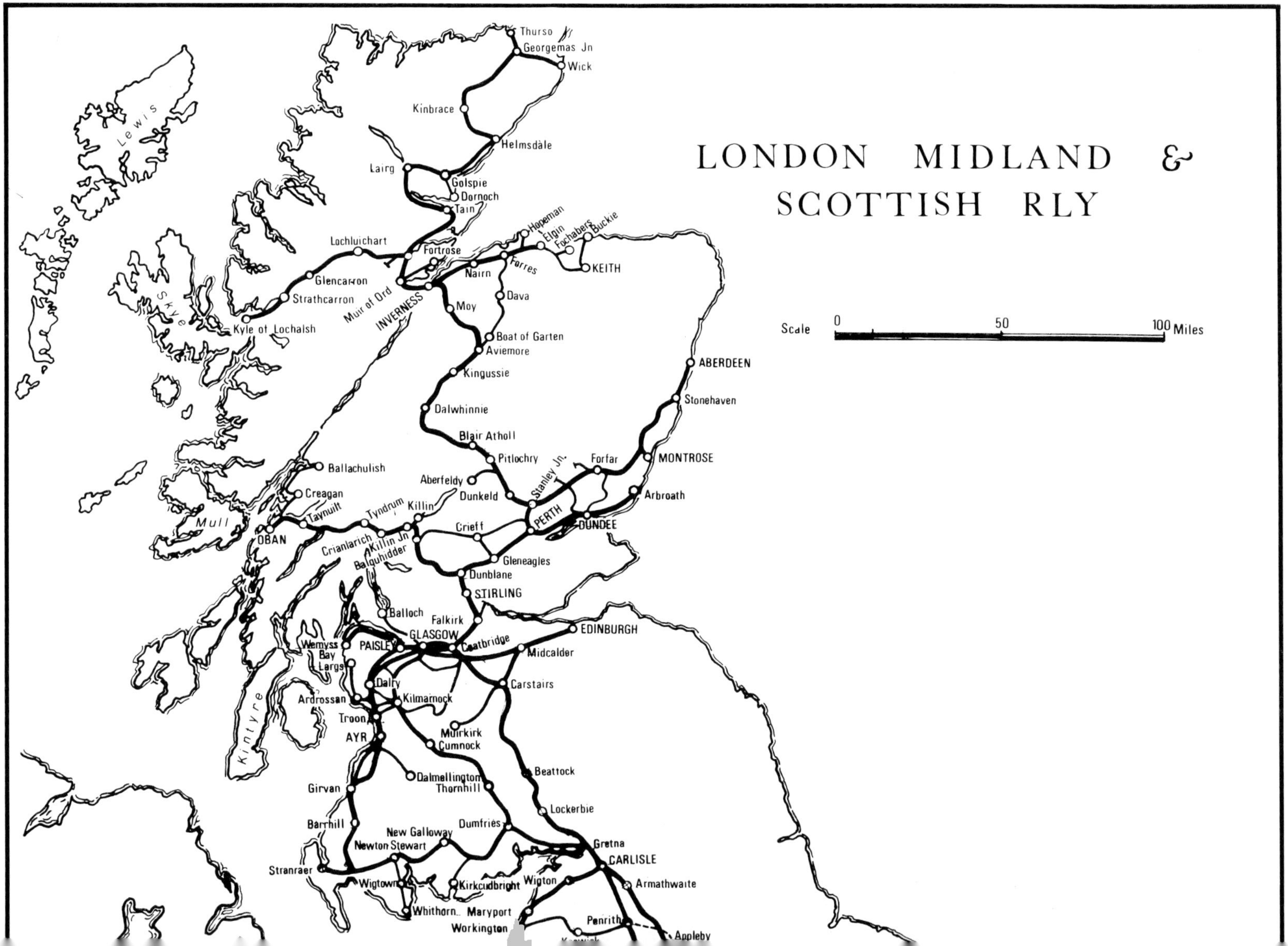

LONDON MIDLAND &
SCOTTISH RLY
Scale
0
50
100 Miles
Lewis
Skye
Mull
Kintyre
Thurso
Georgemas Jn
Wick
Kinbrace
Helmsdale
Lairg
Golspie
Dornoch
Tain
Lochluichart
Fortrose
Glencarron
Strathcarron
Kyle of Lochalsh
Muir of Ord
INVERNESS
Hopeman
Elgin
Fochabers
Buckie
KEITH
Nairn
Forres
Dava
Moy
Boat of Garten
Aviemore
Kingussie
Dalwhinnie
Blair Atholl
Pitlochry
ABERDEEN
Stonehaven
MONTROSE
Forfar
Stanley Jn.
Arbroath
Ballachulish
Aberfeldy
Dunkeld
PERTH
DUNDEE
Creagan
Taynuilt
Tyndrum
Killin
OBAN
Crianlarich
Killin Jn
Balquhidder
Crieff
Gleneagles
Dunblane
STIRLING
Balloch
Falkirk
EDINBURGH
Wemyss Bay
PAISLEY
GLASGOW
Coatbridge
Midcalder
Largs
Dalry
Carstairs
Ardrossan
Kilmarnock
Troon
AYR
Muirkirk
Cumnock
Beattock
Dalmellington
Thornhill
Girvan
Lockerbie
Barrhill
New Galloway
Dumfries
Newton Stewart
Gretna
CARLISLE
Stranraer
Wigtown
Kirkcudbright
Wigton
Armathwaite
Whithorn
Maryport
Workington
Penrith
Appleby

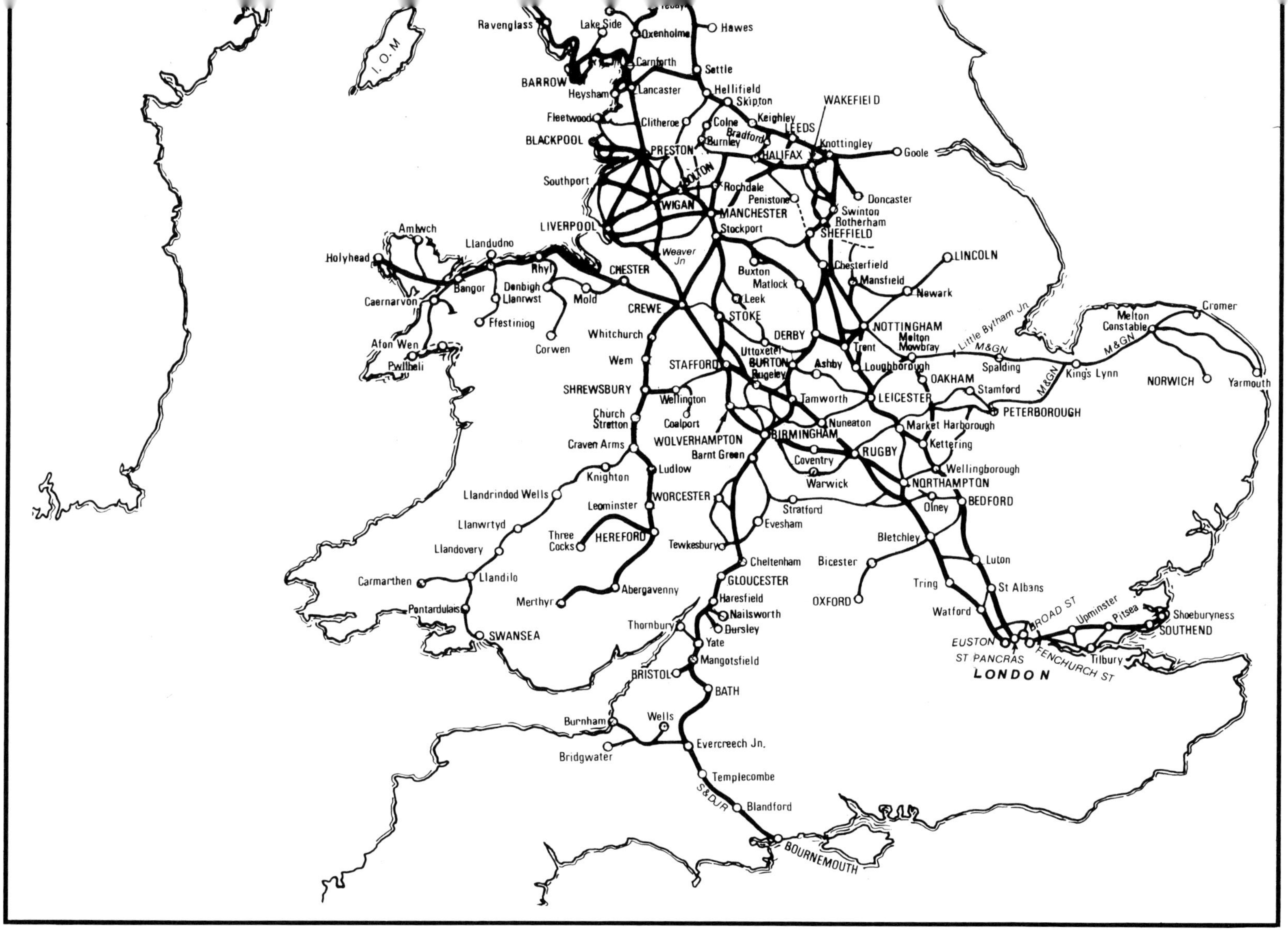

Ravenglass
Lake Side
Oxenholme
Hawes
I.O.M
Carnforth
Settle
BARROW
Heysham
Lancaster
Hellifield
Skipton
WAKEFIELD
Fleetwood
Clitheroe
Colne
Keighley
Bradford
LEEDS
BLACKPOOL
PRESTON
Burnley
HALIFAX
Knottingley
Goole
BOLTON
Southport
Rochdale
Penistone
Doncaster
WIGAN
MANCHESTER
Swinton
Rotherham
LIVERPOOL
Stockport
SHEFFIELD
Amlwch
Llandudno
Holyhead
Weaver Jn
Rhyl
CHESTER
Chesterfield
LINCOLN
Buxton
Bangor
Denbigh
Matlock
Mansfield
Llanrwst
Mold
Newark
Caernarvon
Leek
CREWE
Ffestiniog
STOKE
Little Bytham Jn.
Cromer
Melton Constable
NOTTINGHAM
Whitchurch
DERBY
Corwen
Melton Mowbray
Afon Wen
M&GN
Trent
Uttoxeter
Pwllheli
Wem
BURTON
Ashby
Loughborough
Spalding
Kings Lynn
STAFFORD
NORWICH
Yarmouth
Rugeley
OAKHAM
SHREWSBURY
Stamford
Tamworth
LEICESTER
Wellington
PETERBOROUGH
Church Stretton
Coalport
Nuneaton
Market Harborough
WOLVERHAMPTON
BIRMINGHAM
Craven Arms
Barnt Green
RUGBY
Kettering
Coventry
Ludlow
Wellingborough
Knighton
Warwick
NORTHAMPTON
Llandrindod Wells
WORCESTER
Leominster
Stratford
Olney
BEDFORD
Llanwrtyd
Evesham
Three Cocks
HEREFORD
Bletchley
Llandovery
Tewkesbury
Cheltenham
Bicester
Luton
Carmarthen
Llandilo
GLOUCESTER
Tring
St Albans
Abergavenny
Merthyr
Haresfield
OXFORD
Watford
BROAD ST
Upminster
Pontardulais
Nailsworth
Pitsea
Shoeburyness
Thornbury
Dursley
SOUTHEND
SWANSEA
Yate
EUSTON
ST PANCRAS
FENCHURCH ST
Tilbury
Mangotsfield
LONDON
BRISTOL
BATH
Burnham
Wells
Evercreech Jn.
Bridgwater
Templecombe
S&DJR
Blandford
BOURNEMOUTH

10.00 Euston-Glasgow (The 'Royal Scot')

1927
Euston dep 10.00

BV	C1	O1	KC	O3	O3	C3	C3	B3	B1	O1	KC	O3	C3	B3

Brake Van
Corr First (33)
Open First (36)
Kitchen Car
Open Third (42)
Open Third (42)
Corr Third (64)
Corr Third (64)
Corr Brake Third (40)
} Glasgow

Corr Brake First (27)
Open First (36)
Kitchen Car
Open Third (42)
Corr Third (64)
Corr Brake Third (40)
} Edinburgh

Up working: Glasgow dep 10.00

1930
Euston dep 10.00

BV	O3	O3	O3	O3	KC	O1	B1	B1	C1	KC	O3	O3	B1

Brake Van — Steel
Open Third (56)
Open Third (56)
Open Third (42)
Open Third (42)
Kitchen Car
Semi-Open First (30)
Corr Brake First (16)
} Glasgow

Corr Brake First Lounge (10)
Open Semi-First (30)
Kitchen Car
Open Third (42)
Open Third (56)
Corr Brake First (16)
} Edinburgh

Up working: Glasgow dep 10.00

1934
Euston dep 10.00

B3	C3	C3	C3	O3	O3	KC	O1	B1	BC	O1	KC	O3	C3	B3

Corr Brake Third (24)
Corr Third (42)
Corr Third (42)
Corr Third (42)
Open Third (42) 60ft
Open Third (42) 60ft
Kitchen Car
Semi-Open First (30)
Corr Brake First (16)
} Glasgow

Corr Composite Brake (6/21)
Semi-Open First (30)
Kitchen Car
Open Third 60ft
Corr Third (42)
Corr Brake Third (24)
} Edinburgh

Up working: Glasgow dep 10.00

1949
Euston dep 10.00

B3	C3	O3	KC	O1	C1	C1	B3	B3	C3	CC	CC	C3	B3

Corr Brake Third (24)
Corr Third (42)
Open Third (42)
Kitchen Car
Open First (42)
Corr First (33)
Corr First (33)
Corr Brake Third (24)
} Glasgow

Corr Brake Third (24)
Corr Third (42)
Corr Composite (18/24)
Corr Composite (18/24)
Corr Third (42)
Corr Brake Third (24)
} Edinburgh*

*from Birmingham dep 11.15 — attached at Crewe
LMS stock

Up working: Glasgow dep 10.00

1954

Euston dep 10.00

B3	C3	C3	C3	C3	O3	O3	R3	KC	R1	C1	CC	BV

Corr Brake Third
Corr Third
Corr Third
Corr Third
Corr Third
Open Third
Open Third
Restaurant Open Third
Kitchen Car
Restaurant Open First
Corr First
Corr Composite
Brake Van

BR Mk 1 stock
Up working: Glasgow dep 10.00

1963

Euston dep 09.50

B2	C2	C2	C2	C2	C2	C2	O2	KB	R1	C1	B1

Corr Brake Second
Corr Second
Corr Second
Corr Second
Corr Second
Corr Second
Corr Second
Open Second
Kitchen Buffet
Restaurant Open First
Corr First
Corr Brake First

BR Mk 1 stock
Up working: Glasgow dep 10.00

1973

Euston dep 10.05

B1	O2	O2	O2	O2	O2	O2	RB	O1	C1	C1	BV

Corr Brake First
Tourist Open Second
Tourist Open Second
Tourist Open Second
Tourist Open Second
Tourist Open Second
Tourist Open Second
Restaurant Buffet (23)
Open First
Corr First
Corr First
Brake Van

BR Mk 2 air-braked stock
Up working: Glasgow dep 18.00 to Manchester/ Liverpool

1983

Euston dep 09.45

O2	O2	O2	O2	O2	RB	O1	O1	BV

Tourist Open Second
Tourist Open Second
Tourist Open Second
Tourist Open Second
Tourist Open Second
Restaurant Unclassified Buffet (17)
Open First
Open First
Brake Van

BR Mk 3 stock
Up working: Glasgow dep 17.10

Prior to 1925, the 10.00 from Euston had carried through coaches for Glasgow, Edinburgh, Dundee and Aberdeen. From March 1925 the train ran to Glasgow only, the remainder of the through coaches leaving at 10.08. The 10.00 was christened the 'Royal Scot' in July 1927 and carried portions for Edinburgh and Glasgow, the train being divided at Symington. The formation consisted of modern LMS stock. A Kitchen Car, with partner Open First and Open Third Cars, was allocated to each portion. First Class accommodation was changed the following year. A Lounge Brake First and Semi-Open First replaced the vehicles ahead of the Kitchen Car in both portions. New Period 2 stock was incorporated into the train in 1930, but by 1933 Period 3 vehicles had started to appear. There was little change during the next four years but in 1938 a Corridor Third was added to the rear of the Glasgow portion. In addition the Edinburgh portion was modified to have the following formation: Open Third (42), Kitchen Car, Semi-Open First (30), Open Third (42), Corridor Brake Third (24). All the Third Class coaches in the formation were now Period 3 designs but the First Class vehicles had remained of the older style. A detailed review of the formations in LMS days was given in the April 1979 *Railway World*. After the war the first significant event was the selection of the 'Royal Scot' to participate in the 1948 experimental livery programme. One set was painted carmine and cream while the other received chocolate and cream. The next major change was in 1951 when the train became one of the first to be totally formed of the new BR standard stock, including the new Restaurant Car sets. The formation remained basically the same for several years. There were some changes in the formation by 1960, when an LMS Kitchen Car was being used again. This situation did not last for long and the 1963 formation gave a foretaste of what was to be used for the next 20 years. During the early 1970s when Mk 2 air-braked stock was employed, the down set formed the 18.00 Glasgow-Manchester/Liverpool. The set returned the following morning to form the 13.55 Glasgow-Euston. When the train was changed over to Mk 2 air-conditioned stock in 1974 only one set was used which made a round trip to Glasgow and back in the day. By 1978 the set was formed from Mk 3 coaches.

Right:
The first non-stop run from Euston to Glasgow took place on 27 April 1928. 'Royal Scot' 4-6-0 No 6113 *Cameronian*, fitted with a specially converted high-capacity tender, was in charge of the train which is seen here climbing Beattock Summit. *Real Photos*

Below:
The down 'Royal Scot' at Shap in June 1928 made up of Period 1 LMS stock. 'Royal Scot' 4-6-0 No 6108 *Seaforth Highlander* is in charge. *L. J. Thompson*

Left:
'Royal Scot' 4-6-0 No 6136 *Goliath* takes water at Tebay troughs while working the up 'Royal Scot' on 22 June 1928. *L. J. Thompson*

Below left:
In 1951 the 'Royal Scot' was one of the first trains to be completely made up of BR standard stock. One of the new sets is shown on the outskirts of London behind Stanier 'Duchess' Pacific No 46230 *Duchess of Buccleuch*, the non-streamlined version of the 'Coronation' class built for the 'Coronation Scot'.
Real Photographs 24154

Bottom:
Thirty years later the 'Royal Scot' looked like this. The 08.45 Euston-Glasgow, made up of Mk 3 stock (apart from a rear First) near Tebay in May 1981 is hauled by Class 86/2 No 86227 *Sir Henry Johnson* with crossed-arm pantograph.
J. E. Oxley

10.08 Euston-Stranraer/Perth/Aberdeen

1925
Euston dep 10.08

BC	O1	R1	O3	B3	B3	CC	BC

Vehicle	Destination
Corr Brake Composite (12/32)	Edinburgh
Open First (36)	Edinburgh
Restaurant First (20)	Edinburgh
Open Third (42)	Edinburgh
Corr Brake Third (40)	Edinburgh
Corr Brake Third (40)	Aberdeen
Corr Composite (18/32)	Aberdeen
Corr Brake Composite	

Up working: Aberdeen dep 06.45

1934
Euston dep 10.05

B3	BV	CC	B3	CC	RC	C3	C3	BV	CC	BC	CC	B3

Vehicle	Destination
Corr Brake Third (40) (MO)	Stranraer
Brake Van (MX)	Stranraer
Corr Composite (18/32)	Stranraer
Corr Third Brake (24)	Aberdeen
Corr Composite (18/24)	Aberdeen
Restaurant Composite	Perth
Corr Third (42) (FO)	Perth
Corr Third (42)	Perth
Brake Van	Perth
Corr Composite (18/24)	Dundee
Corr Brake Composite 60ft	Edinburgh
Corr Composite (18/24)	Glasgow
Corr Brake Third (24)	Glasgow

Up working: Aberdeen dep 06.45

1949
Euston dep 10.20

B3	O3	O3	R3	OC	CC	CC	B1	BV	O3	O3

Vehicle	Destination
Corr Brake Third (24)	Perth
Open Third (56)	Perth
Open Third (56)	Perth
Restaurant Third (30)	Perth
Open Composite (18/18)	Perth
Corr Composite (18/24)	Perth
Corr Composite (18/24)	Perth
Corr Brake First (16)	Perth
Brake Van	
Open Third (56) (FO)	Carlisle
Open Third (56) (FO)	Carlisle

LMS stock
Up working: Perth dep 08.55

1954
Euston dep 10.10

B3	C3	C3	CC	C1	B3	B3	C3	O3	R3	OC	OC	B1

Vehicle	Destination
Corr Brake Third (24) (LMS)	Glasgow
Corr Third (BR1)	Glasgow
Corr Third (BR1)	Glasgow
Corr Composite (BR1)	Glasgow
Corr First (33) (LMS)	Glasgow
Corr Brake Third (24) (LMS)	Glasgow
Corr Brake Third (24) (LMS)	Perth
Corr Third (42) (LMS)	Perth
Open Third (56) (LMS)	Perth
Restaurant Third (30) (LMS)	Perth
Open Composite (18/18) (LMS)	Perth
Open Composite (18/18) (LMS)	Perth
Corr Brake First (27) (LMS)	Perth

Up working: Perth dep 09.00

1963
Euston dep 10.00

B2	C2	O2	O2	RB	C1	B1

Corr Brake Second
Corr Second
Open Second
Open Second (48)
Restaurant Buffet (23)
Corr First
Corr Brake First
} Perth

BR Mk 1 stock
Up working: Perth dep 09.00

1983
Euston dep 10.20

UV	UV	BV	O2	O2	O2	O2	O2	O1	O1	RB	O1	B1

General Utility Van
General Utility Van
} Carlisle

Brake Van
Tourist Open Second
Tourist Open Second
Tourist Open Second
Tourist Open Second
Tourist Open Second
Open First
Open First
} Stranraer

Restaurant Buffet (18)
Open First
Corr Brake First
} Carlisle

BR Mk 2 air-conditioned stock
Up working: Stranraer dep 10.38

Until 1925 the Aberdeen coaches were carried on the 10.00 from Euston. Starting in March of that year the 10.00 was divided into two separate trains, the second leaving Euston at 10.08 with through coaches for Aberdeen, Dundee and Edinburgh. The train was made up of coaches to the latest LMS designs apart from the Restaurant Car and the Brake Composite for Dundee which were LNWR vehicles.

The 1927 formation had a portion for Perth, which included a Composite Restaurant Car and a 57ft Open Third. A Brake Composite for Stranraer was carried during the summer. It was transferred at Carlisle to the 16.12 corridor train to Stranraer which consisted of a Brake Third, Open Composite, Restaurant Car (an old Midland & Scottish Joint car which had gone to the G&SWR), and Brake Third. The through coach was located between the latter two vehicles.

New Period 3 stock had appeared in the formation by 1934 but about half the train was made up of older vehicles. The Stranraer portion had gained a Third Class coach by this time, and from Carlisle was accompanied by a modern Composite Restaurant Car. By 1938 the formation had been modified so that the Glasgow portion was at the front of the train, and that for Perth at the rear. Additional vehicles were a Brake Composite for Aberdeen and a Corridor Composite for Dundee, but there was no Edinburgh portion. Period 3 coaches were now used throughout, the Restaurant Car being a 68ft Third partnered by an Open Composite.

After nationalisation the train terminated at Perth, the other destinations having been eliminated. This arrangement continued for a few years but from 1954 the train ran as a combined Perth/Glasgow, composed mainly of LMS stock. During the early electrification work at Euston a portion was carried for Aberdeen instead of Glasgow. In 1963, however, a lightweight set of seven BR standard coaches ran between Euston and Perth. Commencing with the new 1966 timetable the train was retimed to leave at 12.05 with portions for Perth and Glasgow. The Perth service was withdrawn at the end of the 1969 timetable. Stranraer was without a daytime service from London after the war, but in 1980 a new Euston-Stranraer train was introduced with a Restaurant Car to Carlisle.

10.40 Euston-Aberystwyth/Swansea

1923
Euston dep 10.40

B3	CC	CC	B3	RC	BC	C3	BC	BC	RC	B3	BC	CC

Vehicle	Destination
Corr Brake Third 57ft	Manchester
Corr Composite 57ft	Manchester
Corr Composite 57ft	Manchester
Corr Brake Third 57ft	Manchester
Restaurant Composite 65ft	Manchester
Corr Brake Composite 57ft	Halifax
Corr Third 57ft	Colne
Corr Brake Composite (L&Y)	Colne
Corr Brake Composite	Aberystwyth
Restaurant Composite 65ft	Aberystwyth
Corr Brake Third	Aberystwyth
Corr Brake Composite	Llanwrtyd Wells
Corr Composite	Llanwrtyd Wells

LNWR stock
Up working: Aberystwyth dep 08.00

1926
(Euston dep 10.35)
Shrewsbury dep 14.40

BC	BC	C3	BC	BC	C3

Corr Brake Composite 57ft	(ex-Manchester)
Corr Brake Composite 57ft	(ex-Liverpool)
Corr Third 50ft	(ex-Shrewsbury)
Corr Brake Composite 57ft	(ex-Birmingham)
Corr Brake Composite 57ft	(ex-Euston)
Corr Third 57ft (FO)	(ex-Euston)

LNWR stock
Up working: Swansea dep 10.15

1934
Euston dep 10.40

B3	O3	R1	C1	B3	C3	C3	CC	B3	CC	BC

Vehicle	Destination
Corr Brake Third (24)	Liverpool
Open Third 60ft	Liverpool
Restaurant First 65ft	Liverpool
Corr First (36)	Liverpool
Corr Brake Third (24)	Liverpool
Corr Third (42)	Liverpool
Corr Third (42)	Southport
Corr Composite 60ft	Southport
Corr Brake Third (40)	Swansea
Corr Composite (18/32)	Swansea
Corr Brake Composite (12/32)	Swansea

Up working: Swansea dep 07.25

1934
Shrewsbury dep 14.40

T3	C3	BC	BC	BC	CC	B3	BC

Tea Car Third (40)	(ex-Craven Arms)
Corr Third (FO)	(ex-Shrewsbury)
Corr Brake Composite	(ex-Manchester)
Corr Brake Composite	(ex-Liverpool)
Corr Brake Composite (12/32)	(ex-Euston)
Corr Composite (18/32)	(ex-Euston)
Corr Brake Third (40)	(ex-Euston)
Corr Brake Composite	(ex-Stafford)

Up working: Swansea dep 07.35

Before grouping the LNWR ran a complete train from Euston to Swansea and the Welsh Coast, via Stafford and Shrewsbury. For example in 1910, the 11.00 Corridor train included Tri-Composite and Brake Van portions for both Barmouth and Aberystwyth (which had an extra third) along with a Tri-composite brake for Swansea. The Tri-composites for the West Coast were supplied by the Cambrian Railway. A Restaurant Car was carried as far as Stafford.

There were a series of changes after WW1. In 1922 the 11.00 carried an Aberystwyth portion and through coaches for North, Central and South Wales. At grouping there was further modification, the through coaches becoming a portion of the 10.40 Euston-Manchester; a Brake Composite for Swansea left Euston at 13.05. A Restaurant Car was added to the Aberystwyth portion, no doubt to compete with the GWR who had recently introduced similar facilities on their train from Paddington. The Restaurant Car from Euston must have had limited success because in the following year it became a Shrewsbury/Swansea working; the utilisation did not improve, a car being needed in each direction. It appears that the through coaches to Aberystwyth were also withdrawn around this time.

The formation of the train from Euston in June 1926 has been omitted above since only a small part went to South Wales. Instead the train from Shrewsbury onwards is shown. Portions from Manchester, Liverpool and Birmingham, each consisting of a Brake Composite, joined the coaches from Euston. In fact, all four of the Brake Composites were the LNWR type with a brake compartment at each end.

By 1929 a Tea Car had been substituted for the Restaurant Car. This working was cut back soon afterwards to Craven Arms (instead of Shrewsbury) to enable one car to make the round trip. A total of 14 Tea Cars were built by the LNWR in two styles, one having a cove roof and the other an elliptical type.

There was little change during the 1930s, apart from some upgrading of the stock. The make up of the trains in 1934 is typical of this period, the formations from both Euston and Shrewsbury being shown.

While the Swansea service was not reinstated under BR, a Euston-Aberystwyth Saturdays Only train reappeared over 20 years ago and has continued ever since.

10.40 Euston-Blackpool

1934

Euston dep 10.40

OC	R3	BC	BC	BC	C3	BV	C3	C3	BC	C3	B3	CC

Vehicle	Portion
Open Composite	
Restaurant Third 65ft	Carlisle
Corr Brake Composite 60ft	
Corr Brake Composite 60ft	Windermere
Corr Brake Composite (12/32)	
Corr Third (42)	Barrow
Brake Van	
Corr Third (64) (MO)	
Corr Third (64) (MO)	Blackpool
Corr Brake Composite (12/32)	
Corr Third (42)	
Corr Brake Third (24)	Llandudno
Corr Composite (12/32)	

Up working: Blackpool dep 12.25

1949

Euston dep 10.57

CC	O3	CC	B3	B3	O3	O3	R3	O1	CC	CC	B3	O3	CC	B3

Vehicle	Portion
Corr Composite (18/24)	
Open Third (56)	
Corr Composite (18/24)	
Corr Brake Third (24)	
Corr Brake Third (24)	
Open Third (56)	
Open Third (56)	
Restaurant Third (30)	
Open First (42)	
Corr Composite (18/24)	
Corr Composite (18/24)	
Corr Brake Third (24)	
Open Third (56)	
Corr Composite (18/24)	Preston
Corr Brake Third (24)	

LMS stock

Up working: Blackpool dep 08.32

1954

Euston dep 10.50

B3	C3	O3	R3	O1	CC	CC	B3	C3	CC	B3	C3	C3

Vehicle	Portion
Corr Brake Third (24) (LMS)	
Corr Third (42) (LMS)	
Open Third (56) (LMS)	
Restaurant Third (30) (LMS)	
Open First (42) (LMS)	
Corr Composite (BR1)	
Corr Composite (BR1)	
Corr Brake Third (24)	
Corr Third (42) (LMS)	
Corr Composite (18/24) (LMS)	
Corr Brake Third (24)	
Corr Third (42) (LMS) (MFO)	Preston
Corr Third (42) (LMS) (MFO)	

Up working: Blackpool dep 10.00

1963

Euston dep 10.50

B3	MB	CC	CC	C3	B3	C3	C3	B3	CC	B3

Vehicle	Portion
Corr Brake Third (24) (LMS)	
Miniature Buffet (BR)	
Corr Composite (BR)	
Corr Composite (BR)	
Corr Third (BR)	
Corr Brake Third (24) (LMS)	
Corr Third (42) (LMS) (MFO)	
Corr Third (42) (LMS) (MFO)	
Corr Brake Third (24) (LMS)	
Corr Composite (18/24) (LMS)	Preston
Corr Brake Third (24) (LMS)	

Up working: Blackpool dep 07.45

1973

Euston dep 09.00

BV	C3	O2	O2	O2	B1	C1	C1	RB	O1	O2	O2	BV

Brake Van
Corr Third
Tourist Open Second
Tourist Open Second
Tourist Open Second
Corr Brake First
} Carlisle

Corr First
Corr First
Restaurant Buffet (12)
Open First
Tourist Open Second
Tourist Open Second
Brake Van
} Blackpool

BR dual-heated 100mph stock
Up working: Blackpool dep 15.22

1975

Euston dep 11.00

B2	O2	O2	O2	O2	RB	O1	O1	C1	C1	B1

Open Brake Second
Tourist Open Second
Tourist Open Second
Tourist Open Second
Tourist Open Second
Restaurant Buffet (18)
Open First
Open First
Corr First
Corr First
Corr Brake First

BR Mk 2 air-braked stock
Up working: Blackpool dep 15.22

1983

Euston dep 10.40

B2	O2	O2	O2	O2	RB	O1	O1	O1	O1	BV

Brake Second Open
Tourist Open Second
Tourist Open Second
Tourist Open Second
Tourist Open Second
Restaurant Buffet (18)
Open First
Open First
Open First
Open First
Brake Van

BR Mk 2 air-conditioned stock
Up working: Blackpool dep 18.23

In pre-WW2 days the mid-morning service to Blackpool was provided by a through portion and did not run as a separate train except on Saturdays. For example in 1923 the Blackpool portion consisted of three coaches (Corridor Third, Corridor Composite, Brake Corridor Composite) in the 11.35 Euston-Windermere. This had been reduced to a Brake Composite and a Third in 1934, when the pair were carried by the 10.40 Euston-Carlisle.

After the war, a set, including a Restaurant Third, went to Blackpool during the summer timetable, two or three coaches being detached at Preston. BR standard vehicles began to appear in the set by the mid-1950s but LMS stock still represented a significant proportion of the train as late as 1963. After the Euston electrification there was a return to the prewar practice of running a combined Blackpool/Carlisle trains except this time the Restaurant Car went to Blackpool. From 1974 the train became a separate working again and, now made up of Mk 2 air-braked stock, it made two round trips a day between London and Blackpool, leaving Blackpool at 06.20 and 15.22 and Euston at 11.00 and 20.35. The daily circuit of 906 miles was one of the highest on the London Midland Region. In 1978 the working was changed with the morning down train being formed from a Mk 2 air-conditioned set which started the day as the 07.00 from Wolverhampton. There has been little change since then, the set returning to Wolverhampton as the 23.20 from Euston.

11.15 Euston-North Wales (The 'Welshman')

1934
Euston dep 11.15

BC	C3	C3	BC	C3	BC	B3	CC	O1	KC	O3	B3

Vehicles	Destination
Corr Brake Composite 60ft Corr Third (42)	Pwllheli
Corr Third (42) Corr Brake Composite 60ft	Portmadoc
Corr Third (42) (MFO) Corr Brake Composite 60ft	Bangor
Corr Brake Third (24) Corr Composite (18/24) Open First 60ft Kitchen Car Open Third 60ft Corr Brake Third (24)	Llandudno

Up working: Bangor dep 11.20

1949
Euston dep 11.15

B3	O3	O3	CC	BC	R3	O1	B3	CC	CC	B3	O3	CC	B3

Vehicles	Destination
Corr Brake Third (24) Open Third (56) Open Third (56) Corr Composite (18/24) Corr Brake Composite (12/21) Restaurant Third (30) Open First (33)	Holyhead
Corr Brake Third (24) Corr Composite (18/24)	Portmadoc
Corr Composite (18/24) Corr Brake Third (24)	Pwllheli
Open Third (56) Corr Composite (18/24) Corr Brake Third (24)	Llandudno

LMS stock
Up working: Holyhead dep 11.50

1954
Euston dep 11.15

B3	CC	B3	CC	B3	CC	R1	O3	CC	C3	C3	B3

Vehicles	Destination
Corr Brake Third Corr Composite	Portmadoc
Corr Brake Third Corr Composite	Pwllheli
Corr Brake Third Corr Composite Restaurant First (24) (LMS) Open Third (56) (LMS)	Bangor
Corr Composite Corr Third Corr Third Corr Brake Third	Llandudno

BR Mk 1 stock
Up working: Bangor dep 12.45

1963
Euston dep 11.15

B2	CC	B2	CC	O2	KB	BC	CC	C2	C2	CC	B2

Vehicles	Destination
Corr Brake Second Corr Composite	Portmadoc
Corr Brake Second Corr Composite	Pwllheli
Open Second (48) Kitchen/Buffet Corr Brake Composite Corr Composite Corr Second	Holyhead
Corr Second Corr Composite Corr Brake Second	Llandudno

BR Mk 1 stock
Up working: Holyhead dep 11.00

1973
Euston dep 10.15

O2	O2	O2	O2	O2	RB	O1	C1	B1	BV

Tourist Open Second
Tourist Open Second
Tourist Open Second
Tourist Open Second
Tourist Open Second
Restaurant/Buffet (12)
Open First
Corr First
Corr Brake First
Brake Van

BR dual-heated 100mph stock
Up working: Bangor dep 15.28

1983
Euston dep 10.00

O2	B2	O2	O2	O2	O2	O2	RB	O1	O1	O1	BV

Tourist Open Second
Open Brake Second
Tourist Open Second
Tourist Open Second
Tourist Open Second
Tourist Open Second
Tourist Open Second
Restaurant/Buffet (18)
Open First
Open First
Open First
Brake Van

BR Mk 2 air-conditioned stock
Up working: Holyhead dep 01.15

The LMS continued the practice established by the LNWR of rostering a Composite or Brake Composite in each of the four portions carried on this train. The 1934 formation had Brake Composites allocated for the Pwllheli, Portmadoc and Bangor sections, the first two being strengthened with a Third, while Llandudno had a Composite in its six-coach portion. About half the 1934 train was made up of Period 3 stock and in fact this proportion may have been higher since the 60ft Brake Composites could have been of this style. The LNWR practice of providing generous dining accommodation for the train was also continued by the LMS. For example, in 1924 two Restaurant Cars, a First and a Third, and two Open Thirds went to Llandudno. By the end of the 1920s a Kitchen Car with First and Third Open coaches had gone into the train; this requirement remained until WW2. The train returned after the war with a basically similar formation. Main changes, compared to 1934, were the use of Composite/Brake Third pairs for three of the portions and loss of the full Kitchen Car in the dining set, which no longer went to Llandudno.

By 1954 the train was made up of BR standard vehicles apart from the two used for catering. The Bangor portion went on to Holyhead, returning from there to Bangor on the rear of the 11.00 to Manchester. There were few changes to the formation during the next decade. However, by the early 1960s the train only ran during July and August. From 1965, only the Bangor service remained. The 1973 set shown was much more heavily utilised than its predecessors. Returning to Euston the same afternoon, it formed the 21.20 to Holyhead. A couple of years later the 10.00 was extended to Holyhead. Mk 2 air-conditioned stock was used from 1982.

Left:
The northbound 'Welshman' pulls out of Chester behind 'Patriot' 4-6-0 No 45513 in the early 1950s. Note the two 4-wheel Utility Vans behind the locomotive.
J. D. Mills

12.00 Euston-Windermere (The 'Lakes Express')

1923

Euston dep 11.35

BC	C3	B3	CC	RC	BC	BC	BC	CC	B3	C3	CC	BC	RC

Corr Brake Composite
Corr Third } Keswick/Workington

Corr Brake Third
Corr Composite
Restaurant Composite 65ft
Corr Brake Composite } Windermere

Corr Brake Composite
Corr Brake Composite } Whitehaven

Corr Composite (FO)
Corr Brake Third (FO) } Morecambe

Corr Third
Corr Composite
Corr Brake Composite } Blackpool

Restaurant Composite 65ft Preston

LNWR 57ft stock
Up working: Windermere dep 11.25

1934

Euston dep 12.00

BC	CC	O1	KC	O3	B3	B3	CC	BC	C3	BC	O3	BC	BC

Corr Brake Composite 60ft
Corr Composite (18/24)
Open First 60ft
Kitchen Car
Open Third (42)
Corr Brake Third (24) } Windermere

Corr Brake Third (24)
Corr Composite (18/24)
Corr Brake Composite (12/32) } Keswick/ Workington

Corr Third (42)
Corr Brake Composite (12/32) } Whitehaven

Open Third 60ft
Corr Brake Composite (12/32) } Blackpool

Corr Brake Composite (12/32) (FO) Southport

Up working: Windermere dep 11.25

1950

Euston dep 12.00

B3	C3	CC	BC	O3	R1	O3	B3	O3	O3	CC	BC

Corr Brake Third (24)
Corr Third (42)
Corr Composite (18/24)
Corr Brake Composite (12/21)
Open Third 56 (MFO) } Keswick/Workington

Restaurant First (24)
Open Third (56)
Corr Brake Third (24)
Open Third (56)
Open Third (56)
Corr Composite (18/24)
Corr Brake Composite (12/21) } Windermere

LMS stock
Up working: Windermere dep 10.55

1954

Euston dep 11.52

BC	C3	BC	O3	KB	B3	C3	CC	B3	BC	B3	O3	C3	B1

Corr Brake Composite (12/21)
Corr Third (42)
Corr Brake Composite (12/21) } Keswick/Workington

Open Third (56)
Kitchen Buffet
Corr Brake Third (24)
Corr Third (42)
Corr Composite (18/24)
Corr Brake Third (24) } Windermere

Corr Brake Composite (12/21) Barrow

Corr Brake Third (24)
Open Third (56)
Corr Third (42)
Corr Brake First (27) } Whitehaven

LMS stock
Up working: Windermere dep 10.50

1963

Euston dep 11.40

BC	C2	BC	O2	RB	C2	CC	B2	B2	O2	CC	B2	CC

Vehicle	Destination
Corr Brake Composite (12/21) (LMS)	Keswick/ Workington
Corr Second (42) (LMS)	
Corr Brake Composite (12/21) (LMS)	
Open Second (48) (BR1)	Windermere
Restaurant Buffet (23) (BR1)	
Corr Second (BR1)	
Corr Composite (BR1)	
Corr Brake Second (BR1)	
Corr Brake Second (BR1)	Whitehaven
Open Second (BR1)	
Corr Composite (BR1)	
Corr Brake Second (24) (LM)	
Corr Composite (BR1)	Barrow

Up working: Windermere dep 11.05

This summer service had started in LNWR days. For example, in 1910 the 11.30 corridor train from Euston to Scotland carried a Tri-Composite and Brake Van for Keswick, a Third, Tri-Composite and Brake Van for Windermere and a Brake Composite for Whitehaven. Prior to grouping it had become a separate train with a Restaurant Composite to Windermere, and a through portion to Blackpool. The LMS extended the Keswick portion through to Workington and by the late 1920s had increased the dining accommodation by putting in a new Kitchen Car with adjoining Open First and Open Third. The 1934 formation shows a mixture of vehicles from various periods assigned. Brake Composites with 12/32 seating were of LNWR or Period 1 LMS design, and the 60ft Open Thirds represented Period 2. Most of the remainder were Period 3. After WW2 the formation was different. For example, in 1950 there was a portion for Keswick/Workington but the rest of the train, now with a Restaurant First instead of a full Kitchen Car as prewar, went to Windermere. A separate service was provided to Whitehaven. However, by 1954 the Whitehaven portion had been reintroduced (separate trains ran on Saturdays). The formation still consisted of LMS stock at this time, and one of the six Kitchen Buffet Cars (Nos 222-7) which had just been rebuilt at Wolverton from the 1925 batch of Restaurant Composites was at work in the train. During the next few years there was a partial changeover to BR standard stock; the Keswick/Workington portion was still made up from LMS coaches as late as 1963 (they had changed by 1965). Otherwise there were only minor changes in the formation during the last 10 years of the train's existence. Following the West Coast Main Line electrification in 1966 the train ceased to exist.

Left:
A down express with through coaches for the Lake District and a portion from Liverpool is hurried through a cutting near Lancaster by unrebuilt 'Royal Scot' 4-6-0 No 6164.
H. Gordon Tidey

Above:
The Windermere portion of the up 'Lakes Express' crosses over to the up main line at Oxenholme in July 1960. It would then reverse on to the portion from Workington/Penrith waiting at the up platform prior to departing behind Stanier 'Jubilee' class 4-6-0 No 45738 *Samson*. *T. Boustead*

Below:
Class 47 No D1624 passes Preston with a Euston-Windermere service on 10 June 1968. Note the presence of LMS-designed stock towards the rear of the train. *Derek Cross*

13.30 Euston-Glasgow (The 'Midday Scot')

1927
Euston dep 13.30

BC	B3	RC	CC	B3	CC	RC	B3	BC	BV

Vehicle	Destination
Corr Brake Composite (GWR)	Plymouth-Glasgow†
Corr Brake Third (40) Restaurant Composite (15/21) Corr Composite (27/16) Corr Brake Third (40)	Glasgow
Corr Composite (24/24) Restaurant Composite (15/21) Corr Brake Third (32)	Edinburgh
Corr Brake Composite (12/24) Brake Van	Aberdeen

WCJS stock
Up working: Glasgow dep 13.30

1934
Euston dep 13.30

BC	BV	C3	C3	CC	O3	R3	O1	B1	B3	O1	R3	C3	C3	B3

Vehicle	Destination
Corr Brake Composite (GWR)	Plymouth-Glasgow†
Brake Van Steel Corr Third (42) Corr Third (42) Corr Composite (18/32) (MFO) Open Third 60ft Restaurant Third (30) Semi-Open First (30)	Glasgow
Corr Brake First (16) Corr Brake Third (24) Semi-Open First (30) Restaurant Third (30) Corr Third (42) (MFO) Corr Third (42) (FO) Corr Brake Third (24)	Edinburgh

Up working: Glasgow dep 13.30

1938
Euston dep 14.00

B3	O1	R3	O3	B3	BC	CC	B3	CC	B3	BC	C3	CC	B3

Vehicle	Destination
Corr Brake Third (24) Semi-Open First (30) Restaurant Third (30) Open Third (42) Corr Brake Third (24)	Euston-Edinburgh
Corr Brake Composite	Manchester-Edinburgh*
Corr Composite (18/24) Corr Brake Third (24)	Manchester-Glasgow*
Corr Composite (18/24) Corr Brake Third (24)	Euston-Glasgow
Corr Brake Composite (GWR)	Plymouth-Glasgow†
Corr Third (64) (MFO)	Crewe-Glasgow
Corr Composite (18/24) Corr Brake Third (24)	Liverpool-Glasgow**

*Manchester dep 16.45; attached at Wigan
**Liverpool dep 17.00; attached at Lancaster
Up working: Glasgow dep 13.35

1949
Euston dep 13.00

C3	C3	B3	C3	O3	O3	KC	O1	O1	CC	B3	CC	C3	BV

Corr Third (42) (FO)
Corr Third (42) (FO)
Corr Brake Third (24)
Corr Third (42)
Open Third (56)
Open Third (42)
Kitchen Car
Open First (42)
Semi-Open First (30)
Corr Composite (18/24)
Corr Brake Third (24)
Corr Composite (18/24)
Corr Third (42)
Brake Van

LMS stock
Up working: Glasgow dep 13.15

1954
Euston dep 13.30

BC	BV	C3	B3	C3	C3	O3	O3	KC	O1	C1	CC	BV	CC	B3	C3	C3

Corr Brake Composite (12/21) (GWR)*
Brake Van Steel
Corr Third (42) (LM) (MFO)
Corr Brake Third (24) (LM)
Corr Third (BR1)
Corr Third (BR1)
Open Third (BR1)
Open Third (BR1)
Kitchen Car (LM)
Open First (BR1)
Corr First (BR1)
Corr Composite (BR1)
Brake Van (BR1)
Corr Composite (18/24) (LM)
Corr Brake Third (24) (LM)
Corr Third (42) (LM)
Corr Third (42) (LM)
} Carlisle

*Plymouth-Glasgow†
Up working: Glasgow dep 13.30

1963
Euston dep 13.10

B2	C2	C2	C2	O2	KB	O1	CC	C1	B1	C2	BC

Corr Brake Second
Corr Second
Corr Second
Corr Second
Open Second
Kitchen Buffet
Open First
Corr Composite
Corr First
Corr Brake First
Corr Second*
Corr Brake Composite*

*Plymouth-Glasgow†
BR Mk 1 stock
Up working: Glasgow dep 13.30

1973
Euston dep 14.05

BV	O2	O2	O2	O2	O2	O2	O2	RB	O2	C1	B1

Brake Van
Tourist Open Second
Tourist Open Second
Tourist Open Second
Tourist Open Second
Tourist Open Second
Tourist Open Second
Tourist Open Second
Restaurant Buffet Car (23)
Open Second (48)
Corr First
Corr Brake First

BR Mk 2 air-braked stock
Up working: Glasgow dep 10.00

1982
Euston dep 12.45

O2	O2	O2	O2	O2	RB	O1	O1	O1	BV

Tourist Open Second
Tourist Open Second
Tourist Open Second
Tourist Open Second
Tourist Open Second
Unclassified Restaurant Buffet (17)
Open First
Open First
Open First
Brake Van

Mk 3 stock
Up working: Glasgow dep 12.10

†Attached at Crewe

The predecessor of the 'Midday Scot', which received its name in September 1927, was the 14.00 'Corridor' from Euston. Introduced in 1893, 18 coaches had been specifically built for the service in 1908. The formation shown for 1927 (June) was still made up from these vehicles: the Restaurant Composites dated back to 1905. In July of that year the 1908 coaches were withdrawn from the Edinburgh and Aberdeen portions and replaced with standard LMS vehicles: a Composite (18/32) and Brake Third for Edinburgh and a Composite (18/32) and Brake Van for Aberdeen. A similar change was made to the Glasgow portion for the start of the 1927 winter timetable. There were several modifications in the following year including the appearance of a Restaurant First built by the Midland in 1921 in the Glasgow portion. Period 2 coaches began to appear by 1930 including the Semi-Open First type. By the summer of 1934 the formation consisted of Period 2 and 3 stock apart from the Restaurant Cars which were LNWR types. New Restaurant Thirds went into the train later in the year. Following the introduction of the 'Coronation Scot' in July 1937 the character of the 'Midday Scot' was completely changed. This is reflected in the formation shown for 1938. The Glasgow portion from Euston was reduced to two coaches, and through coaches to Scotland from Manchester and Liverpool were added at Wigan and Lancaster respectively. A detailed review of the prewar formations was published in the June and July 1985 issues of *Railway World*.

After nationalisation the train only ran between London and Glasgow. One of the Semi-Open Firsts which had been a feature of the prewar train was retained, but the Restaurant Car working had changed. The 1954 train contained a large proportion of BR standard coaches and now had a load of up to 17 vehicles between Crewe and Carlisle. The through coach between Plymouth and Glasgow, which was attached at Crewe, had reappeared by 1954. As in prewar days a GWR Brake Composite was rostered. Following the start of the Euston electrification work the load was reduced to eight coaches for a while and the Plymouth coaches were taken north on the Perth train. By 1963 the permitted load had increased and the Plymouth portion, now two BR (WR) standard coaches, was again picked up at Crewe. This through working ceased in 1966. Following the 1966 electrification the 'Midday Scot' title was dropped. The early afternoon departure from Euston to Glasgow no longer had any distinguishing features and from 1983 became a weekend working only.

Above left:
The down 'Midday Scot' at Crewe South in the late 1920s. The first three coaches of the Glasgow portion were 65ft vehicles built for the service in 1908. The remainder of the set consisted of LMS-built stock. The locomotive is 'Royal Scot' 4-6-0 No 6112 *Sherwood Forester* in original condition.
Ian Allan Library

Left:
Unrebuilt 'Royal Scot' No 6124 takes water at Tebay while working the first portion of the 'Midday Scot'.

Top right:
The down 'Coronation Scot' passing Kilburn in 1937. New Period 3 stock, modified with special interiors, made up the formation of: B3, 03, KC, 03, 03, KC, 01, C1, B1 behind streamlined 'Coronation' Pacific No 6220 *Coronation*. *E. R. Wethersett*

Centre right:
While electrification was in progress from Weaver Junction to Glasgow, Anglo-Scottish trains were worked over this section by Class 50 diesels. Masts and wiring are already in position at Scout Green, on Shap, as Nos D433 and D409 pass with a Glasgow-Euston express on 28 September 1971. *Derek Cross*

Below:
A modern version of the 'Midday Scot'. The 14.00 Glasgow-Euston, made up of Mk 2 air-conditioned stock behind Class 86/2 No 86 250, calls at Lancaster on the way south. *N. A. Machell*

16.15 Euston-Glasgow (The 'Caledonian')

1958
Euston dep 16.15

B2	O2	O2	O2	KC	O1	O1	B1

Corr Brake Second
Open Second (48)
Open Second (48)
Open Second (48)
Kitchen Car (LMS)
Open First
Open First
Corr Brake First (30) (LMS)

BR Mk 1 stock
Up working: Glasgow dep 16.00

1963
Euston dep 15.45

B2	C2	C2	C2	O2	KB	O1	C1	B1

Corr Brake Second
Corr Second
Corr Second
Corr Second
Open Second
Kitchen Buffet
Open First
Corr First
Corr Brake First

BR Mk 1 stock
Up working: Glasgow dep 08.30

The London Midland Region introduced the 'Caledonian' in the summer of 1957 as a late afternoon express to Glasgow. In the up direction the train departed from Glasgow at 08.30. The eight-coach set was made up of BR standard stock with the exception of the Kitchen Car and a Brake First which were of LMS origin. The Open Seconds were of the 48-seat, rather than 64-seat, type. In the summer of 1958 the train was duplicated, with an identical set, leaving Euston at 07.45. Poor loadings resulted in its withdrawal at the start of the winter timetable. By 1960 a BR standard Brake First had replaced the LMS coach. The Kitchen Car still remained the same but it was changed some time during the next two years to a standard Kitchen Buffet. Also by 1963 there had been a change to the Second Class accommodation, two Open Thirds being replaced by three Corridor Thirds, and the other Open Third changing to the 64-seat type. The service was dropped in the following year.

Left:
The up 'Caledonian' entering Euston. Note the LMS Period 3 Brake First behind the engine which was regularly rostered for the train during the initial years of operation. The locomotive is No 46240 Pacific *City of Coventry* after removal of streamlining. *B. Sackville*

16.35 Euston-Wolverhampton

1923
Euston dep 16.35

B3	C1	B3	RC	C3	B3	CC	B3	C1

Corr Brake Third
Corr First
Corr Brake Third
Restaurant Composite 65ft
Corr Third
Corr Brake Third
Corr Composite
Corr Brake Third
Corr First

LNWR 57ft stock
Up working: Wolverhampton dep 08.03

1934
Euston dep 16.35

B3	C3	OC	R3	C1	CC	B3	C3	BC

Corr Brake Third (24)
Corr Third (64)
Open Composite (18/32)
Restaurant Third (30)
Corr First (36)
Corr Composite (18/24)
Corr Brake Third (24)
Corr Third (42) (FO)
Corr Brake Composite (9/21) Walsall

Up working: Wolverhampton dep 12.25

1949
Euston dep 16.30

C3	C3	B3	O3	O3	O3	B3	OC	OC	O3	O3	O3	O3	O3	O3	KC	O1	O1	CC	B1

Corr Third (42) (FO)
Corr Third (42) (FO)
Corr Brake Third (24)
Open Third (56) } Twin
Open Brake Third (44) }
Open Composite (18/31) } Twin
Open Third (56) }
Open Third (56) } Twin
Open Third (56) }
Kitchen Car
Open First (42)
Semi-Open First (30)
Corr Composite (18/21)
Corr Brake First (18)

LMS stock
Up working: Wolverhampton dep 08.00

1954
Euston dep 16.37

C3	C3	B3	C3	C3	O3	O3	KC	O1	CC	B1

Corr Third (42) (LMS) (FO)
Corr Third (42) (LMS)
Corr Brake Third (BR1)
Corr Third (BR1)
Corr Third (BR1)
Open Third (BR1)
Open Third (BR1)
Kitchen Car (LMS)
Open First (42) (LMS)
Corr Composite (BR1)
Corr Brake First (30) (LMS)

Up working: Wolverhampton dep 11.55

1963

Euston dep 16.30

O2	O2	C2	C2	B2	O2	O2	KB	O1	C1	C1	B2	BV

Open Second (56) (LMS) (MO)
Open Second (56) (LMS)
Corr Second (42) (LMS)
Corr Second
Corr Brake Second
Open Second
Open Second
Kitchen Buffet
Open First
Corr First
Corr First
Corr Brake Second
Brake Van (TO)

BR Mk 1 stock
Up working: Wolverhampton dep 06.47

1973

Euston dep 16.10

B2	O2	O2	O2	O2	RB	O1	O2	O1	O1	O1	BV

Open Brake Second
Tourist Open Second
Tourist Open Second
Tourist Open Second
Tourist Open Second
Restaurant Buffet (12)
Open First
Tourist Open Second
Open First
Open First
Open First
Brake Van

BR Mk 2 air-conditioned stock
Up working: Wolverhampton dep 18.55

1983

Euston dep 16.10

O2	O2	O2	O2	O2	RB	O1	O1	O1	O1	BV	BV

Tourist Open Second
Tourist Open Second
Tourist Open Second
Tourist Open Second
Tourist Open Second
Restaurant Buffet (18)
Open First
Open First
Open First
Open First
Brake Van
Brake Van

BR Mk 2 air-conditioned stock
Up working: Birmingham dep 18.18

This train was established by the LNWR as an afternoon express for businessmen returning to the Midlands. Prior to WW1 there was a through coach, a Tri-Composite, for Melton Mowbray. The 1923 formation would have been made up of LNWR corridor stock; specific sets were allocated to the Wolverhampton services at this time. Some 10 years later, the set consisted primarily of LMS Period 1 and Period 3 vehicles. One of the new Restaurant Thirds, built in the previous year, being included. The dining capacity then provided by the Restaurant Third and Open Composite pair must have been insufficient as the arrangement was soon changed to Restaurant Third, Open First and Open Third.

The formation shown for 1949 contained three pairs of articulated coaches (Twin-Sets). They were built in 1937, as members of 10-coach articulated sets of open stock. Because of operating restrictions, the 11 sets built had been allocated, before the war, to the Central Division of the LMS. The other five Euston-Wolverhampton sets contained at least two pairs of the Twins in 1949. Three pairs were still in the 16.30 Wolverhampton train the following summer, but by 1954 they had been displaced by new BR vehicles. The dining accommodation of the postwar set had changed to a full Kitchen Car paired with an Open First and two Open Thirds. This arrangement was continued in the 1960s, but with a Mk 1 Kitchen Buffet. From then on there has been little change to the basic make-up of the train. Air-conditioned stock took over the service in the early 1970s.

18.00 Euston-Manchester (The 'Lancastrian')

1923
Euston dep 18.05

B3	**CC**	**O3**	**R1**	**B1**	**BC**	**BC**	**CC**	**BC**

Corr Brake Third
Corr Composite
Restaurant Open Third
Restaurant First
Corr Brake First
Corr Brake Composite 57ft — Halifax
Corr Brake Composite 54ft* } Colne
Corr Composite* } Colne
Corr Brake Composite* — Rochdale

MR stock
*L&Y stock
Up working: Manchester dep 12.05

1926
Euston dep 18.05

B3	**CC**	**O3**	**O3**	**KC**	**O1**	**B1**	**RC**	**BC**	**BC**	**BC**

Corr Brake Third
Corr Composite
Open Third
Open Third
Kitchen Car
Open First
Corr Brake First
Restaurant Composite 65ft
Corr Brake Composite — Halifax
Corr Brake Composite — Colne
Corr Brake Composite — Rochdale

57ft stock
Up working: Manchester dep 12.05

1934
Euston dep 18.00

B3	**O3**	**O3**	**KC**	**O1**	**CC**	**CC**	**B1**	**RC**	**O3**	**C3**	**C3**

Corr Brake Third (24)
Open Third (56)
Open Third (42)
Kitchen Car
Open First (42)
Corr Composite (18/24)
Corr Composite (18/24)
Corr Brake First (27)
Restaurant Composite (12/18)
Open Third (56)
Corr Third (42)
Corr Third (42) (FO)

Up working: Manchester dep 12.05

1949
Euston dep 18.00

B3	**O3**	**O3**	**O3**	**O3**	**OC**	**KC**	**O1**	**O1**	**BC**	**C1**	**C3**	**CC**	**CC**	**B3**

Corr Brake Third (24)
Open Third (56)
Open Third (56)
Open Third (56)
Open Third (56)
Open Composite (18/18)
Kitchen Car
Open First (42)
Open First (42)
Corr Brake Composite (12/21)
Corr First (36)
Corr Third (42)
Corr Composite (18/24) } Colne
Corr Composite (18/24) } Colne
Corr Brake Third (24) } Colne

LMS stock
Up working: Manchester dep 09.45

1954

Euston dep 18.00

B3	**C3**	**C3**	**O3**	**O3**	**OC**	**KC**	**O1**	**O1**	**B3**	**C1**	**C1**	**C3**	**C3**	**B1**

Corr Brake Third (BR1)
Corr Third (BR1)
Corr Third (BR1)
Open Third (BR1)
Open Third (BR1)
Open Composite (18/18) (LMS)
Kitchen Car (LMS)
Open First (42) (LMS)
Open First (42) (LMS)

Corr Brake Third (BR1)
Corr First (BR1)
Corr First (BR1)
Corr Third (42) (LMS) }
Corr Third (42) (LMS) } Colne
Corr Brake First (30) (LMS) }

Up working: Manchester dep 09.45

1963

Euston dep 18.05

B2	**CC**	**CC**	**C2**	**O2**	**O2**	**O2**	**KC**	**O1**	**O1**	**C1**	**B2**

Corr Brake Second
Corr Composite
Corr Composite
Corr Second
Open Second
Open Second (48)
Open Second (48)
Kitchen Car

Open First
Open First
Corr First
Corr Brake Second

BR Mk 1 stock
Up working: Manchester dep 09.40

1973

Euston dep 17.35

B2	**O2**	**O2**	**O2**	**O2**	**O2**	**KB**	**O1**	**O1**	**C1**	**C1**	**B1**

Open Brake Second
Tourist Open Second
Tourist Open Second
Tourist Open Second
Tourist Open Second
Tourist Open Second
Kitchen Buffet Car
Open First

Open First
Corr First
Corr First
Corr Brake First

BR Mk 2 air conditioned stock
Up working: Manchester dep 07.00

1983

Euston dep 18.10

B2	**O2**	**O2**	**O2**	**O2**	**KB**	**O1**	**O1**	**O1**	**BV**

Open Brake Second
Tourist Open Second
Tourist Open Second
Tourist Open Second
Tourist Open Second
Kitchen Buffet Car
Open First

Open First
Open First
Brake Van

BR Mk 3 stock
Up working: Manchester dep 07.00

The LNWR provided extensive dining facilities for its passengers on the 18.00 to Manchester. In 1910 half of the six-coach set was given over to catering. This emphasis was continued by the LMS, no less than five vehicles being assigned by the mid-1920s. They consisted of a Kitchen Car, operating with an Open First and two Open Thirds, and a separate Restaurant Composite.

Immediately after grouping the train must have undergone a transformation as the summer 1923 Carriage Working book shows the Manchester coaches as Midland stock. Lancashire & Yorkshire Railway vehicles were specified for the through working to Colne and Rochdale. Apparently the Midland coaches were removed in 1926, being replaced by 57ft vehicles which could have been of LNWR or LMS origin. Also by this time, the through coaches to Colne etc were LNWR Brake Composites with a brake compartment at each end.

There were six catering vehicles by 1934, an Open Third (Period 1 or 2) having joined the Restaurant Composite. The latter was specified to be a 'new type'. The Open Thirds partnering the Kitchen Car were 60ft Period 2 vehicles. Most of the other vehicles in the formation were of Period 3 design. However, the Manchester part of the train had grown to such a degree that the through coaches for other destinations left Euston on the Heysham train.

While extensive dining accommodation reappeared in the postwar period, five vehicles being assigned (two Open Firsts, a Kitchen Car, an Open Composite and an Open Third), the second Restaurant Car was missing. A portion for Colne also reappeared. New BR standard coaches soon went into the train; the 1954 set only had LMS vehicles in the dining and Colne portions. During the second half of the 1950s the second Restaurant Car finally returned, an LMS Third being used. This arrangement lasted for a few years but by 1963 BR standard stock was used throughout with the cooking concentrated in a BR Kitchen Car. Following the 1966 electrification the 18.00 Manchester Pullman abstracted the First Class clientele, but an ordinary train ran 30min earlier. By the mid-1970s it had returned almost to its old departure time.

Above right:
The down 'Mancunian' from Euston to Manchester, consisting of six coaches, soon after grouping. The leading Brake Third was one of the LNWR 'Toplight' series of elliptical roof coaches, followed by an LMS-built Corridor Third. The next vehicle appears to be one of the Restaurant Composites built in 1925, and was partnered with a contemporary Open coach. Motive power is LNW 'Claughton' class 4-6-0 No 5991.
Real Photographs T8138

Right:
The same Manchester-bound train in early BR days. The train now consisted mainly of Period 3 stock but there were a few Period 1 coaches present. The leading Brake Third was one of the postwar production series. Rebuilt 'Royal Scot' 4-6-0 No 46121 *Highland Light Infantry, City of Glasgow Regiment* is in charge. *E. R. Wethersett*

18.05 Euston-Liverpool (The 'Merseyside Express')

1926

Euston dep 17.55

CC	B3	C1	R1	O1	O3	KC	O3	C3	B3	B1	C3

Corr Composite (MFO)
Corr Brake Third (40)
Corr First (36)
Restaurant First 65ft
Open First (24)
Open Third (42)
Kitchen Car
Open Third (42)
Corr Third (56)
Corr Brake Third (40)
Corr Brake First (12) } Southport
Corr Third (56) }

Up working: Liverpool dep 09.40

1934

Euston dep 18.05

B3	CC	B1	O1	R1	CC	CC	O3	KC	O3	B3	C3	C3	B1

Corr Brake Third (24)
Corr Composite (18/24)
Open Brake First Lounge (10)
Open First 60ft
Restaurant First
Corr Composite (18/24)
Corr Composite (18/24)
Open Third 60ft
Kitchen Car
Open Third 60ft
Corr Brake Third (24)
Corr Third (64) (FO)
Corr Third (42) } Southport
Corr Brake First (27) }

Up working: Liverpool dep 10.00

1949

Euston dep 17.45

C3	B3	CC	CC	O3	O3	KC	O1	O1	C1	B3	C3	CC	BC

Corr Third (42) (FO)
Corr Brake Third (24)
Corr Composite (18/24)
Corr Composite (18/24)
Open Third (56)
Open Third (56)
Kitchen Car
Open First (42)
Open First (42)
Corr First (33)
Corr Brake Third (24)
Corr Third (42)
Corr Composite (18/24)
Corr Brake Composite (12/21)

LMS stock

Up working: Liverpool dep 10.00

1954

Euston dep 18.10

B3	C3	CC	O3	O3	KC	O1	O1	C1	B3	C3	C3	CC	B3

Corr Brake Third
Corr Third
Corr Composite
Open Third (56) (LMS)
Open Third (56) (LMS)
Kitchen Car (LMS)
Open First
Open First
Corr First
Corr Brake Third
Corr Third
Corr Third }
Corr Composite } Southport
Corr Brake Third }

BR Mk 1 stock

Up working: Liverpool dep 10.10

1963

Euston dep 18.17

B2	C2	CC	MB	O2	O2	KC	O1	C1	B2	O2	B2

Corr Brake Second
Corr Second
Corr Composite
Miniature Buffet
Open Second
Open Second (48)
Kitchen Car
Open First
Corr First
Corr Brake Second
Open Second } Southport
Corr Brake Second }

BR Mk 1 stock
Up working: Liverpool dep 10.10

1973

Euston dep 18.30

BV	O2	O2	O2	O2	O2	KB	O1	O1	C1	C1	B1

Brake Van
Tourist Open Second
Tourist Open Second
Tourist Open Second
Tourist Open Second
Tourist Open Second
Kitchen Buffet Car
Open First
Open First
Corr First
Corr First
Corr Brake First

BR Mk 2 air-conditioned stock
Up working: Liverpool dep 07.00

1983

Euston dep 18.00

B2	O2	O2	O2	O2	KB	O1	O1	O1	O1	BV

Open Brake Second
Tourist Open Second
Tourist Open Second
Tourist Open Second
Tourist Open Second
Kitchen Buffet Car
Open First
Open First
Open First
Open First
Brake Van

BR Mk 3 air-conditioned stock
Up working: Liverpool dep 07.00

This evening service to Liverpool had started in 1905. Prior to then the train had been combined with both Manchester and Fleetwood portions. Dining facilities were a feature of the service; in 1910 four out of the eight vehicles were for dining. This was continued by the LMS. Initially the 68ft Pantry Thirds were represented in the set, these being the only 68ft catering cars built by the LNWR. The set was mainly made up of new LMS-built stock by 1926. Third Class dining was in two new Open Thirds served by a Kitchen Car, while First Class diners were seated in a LNWR Restaurant Car and a new Open First. Two LNWR coaches were carried for Southport, being transferred to Edge Hill.

Similar facilities existed in the formation shown for 1934 but with updated stock. A new First Class Restaurant Car had gone into the set together with Open First and Open Thirds of Period 2 design. The First Class brake lounge included in the set was one of five built in 1928 for the 'Royal Scot'. Although fitted with leather armchairs and settees for 10 passengers they were not popular. The remainder of the coaches in the 1934 Liverpool set were of Period 3 style.

British Railways continued to provide extensive dining facilities in the form of two Open Firsts and two Open Thirds served from a central Kitchen Car. Following the appearance of BR standard coaches the set, except for the dining portion, was soon changed over to this type of stock. There was little change to the formation during the next 10 years.

A Miniature Buffet Car was added in the early 1960s but the train loading was reduced because of the West Coast electrification work. When this was completed the 'Liverpool Pullman' took over the time slot and function of the 'Merseyside Express'. There was an 18.30 departure to Liverpool (through coaches to Southport were discontinued) and after the demise of the Pullman this was eventually retimed to depart at 18.00. From 1975 the set has been formed of Mk 3 stock.

Top:
Up 'Merseyside Express' passing Bletchley in about 1933. A Period 3 Brake Third was the second vehicle behind the engine ('Patriot' 4-6-0 No 5987) but the rest of the set appears to consist of earlier style coaches.
Real Photographs T8396

Above:
A Euston-Liverpool express hauled by 'Princess' Pacific No 46206 *Princess Marie Louise* runs beside the M1 between Weedon and Welton in pre-electrification days.
Derek Cross

Manchester and Liverpool Pullmans

The 'Manchester Pullman'

1973
Euston dep 18.00

PB	PC	PK	PC	PC	PK	PC	PB

Parlour Brake
Parlour Car
Parlour Kitchen
Parlour Car
Parlour Car
Parlour Kitchen
Parlour Car
Parlour Brake

Up working: Manchester dep 07.30

1983
Euston dep 16.56

PB	PK	PC	PC	PK	PC	PB

Parlour Brake
Parlour Kitchen
Parlour Car
Parlour Car
Parlour Kitchen
Parlour Car
Parlour Brake

Up working: Manchester dep 07.35

The 'Liverpool Pullman'

1973
Euston dep 17.55

B2	O2	O2	RB	O2	PC	PK	PC	PB

Open Brake Second
Tourist Open Second
Tourist Open Second
Restaurant Buffet (12)
Open Second
Parlour Car
Parlour Kitchen
Parlour Car
Parlour Brake

Up working: Liverpool dep 08.00

For the start of the new electrified service from Euston, 29 new Pullman cars were built at Derby. They consisted of eight 18-seat Parlour Kitchens (M500-7), 14 36-seat Parlour Cars (M540-53) and seven Parlour Brakes (M580-6). Mk 2 bodies were used but Pullman-type interiors and air conditioning were fitted. Two eight-coach sets of Pullman cars were provided for the Manchester service, leaving Euston and Manchester at breakfast time, and returning in the late afternoon. From the mid-1970s both sets have consisted of seven vehicles, a Parlour Car being removed. From 1982 there was a slight difference between the two sets, the leading two coaches behind the brake (leaving Euston) being formed the opposite way round. With the start of the 1985/86 timetable the Pullman cars were removed and a new service, using Mk 2 and 3b coaches, commenced.

Two sets were provided for the Liverpool service but half of each was formed from ordinary BR stock. Departure times were within a few minutes of the Manchester Pullmans. The Liverpool Pullmans were withdrawn from May 1975, but the name returned 10 years later for new services using Mk 3b coaches.

18.10 Euston-Heysham (The 'Ulster Express')

1934

Euston dep 18.10

BV	C3	C3	C3	O3	R1	CC	CC	B1	BC	BC	BC	SV

Brake Van Steel
Corr Third (42) (FO)
Corr Third (42)
Corr Third (42)
Open Third (42)
Restaurant First (24)
Corr Composite (18/24)
Corr Composite (18/24)
Brake First Lounge (10)
Corr Brake Composite (12/32)
Corr Brake Composite 60ft — Colne*
Corr Brake Composite 60ft — Rochdale*
Scenery Van — Holyhead

*Transferred at Crewe to 21.08 to Low Moor
Up working: Heysham dep 05.48

1949

Euston dep 16.45

BV	O3	C3	C3	B3	O3	O3	O3	KC	O1	O1	CC	CC	CC	B1

Brake Van
Open Third (56) (MFO)
Corr Third (42)
Corr Third (42)
Corr Brake Third (24)
Open Third (56)
Open Third (56)
Open Third (56)
Kitchen Car
Open First (42)
Semi-Open First (30)
Corr Composite (18/24)
Corr Composite (18/24)
Corr Composite (18/24)
Corr Brake First

LMS stock
Up working: Heysham dep 06.30

1954

Euston dep 18.20

C3	B3	C3	C3	O3	KC	O1	C1	CC	B3

Corr Third (FO)
Corr Brake Third (24)
Corr Third (BR1)
Corr Third (BR1)
Open Third (BR1)
Kitchen Car (LMS)
Open First (BR1)
Corr First (BR1)
Corr Composite (BR1)
Corr Brake Third (BR1)

Up working: Heysham dep 06.30

1963

Euston dep 17.52

C2	B2	C2	C2	O2	O2	KB	O1	O2	C1	B2

Corr Second (42) (LMS) (MFO)
Corr Brake Second
Corr Second
Corr Second
Open Second
Open Second
Kitchen Buffet
Open First
Open Second
Corr First
Corr Brake Second

BR Mk 1 stock
Up working: Heysham dep 06.55

1974

Euston dep 18.30

B2	O2	O2	O2	O2	O2	KB	O1	C1	C1	B1	BV

Open Brake Second
Tourist Open Second
Tourist Open Second
Tourist Open Second
Tourist Open Second
Tourist Open Second
Kitchen Buffet
Open First
Corr First
Corr First
Corr Brake First
Brake Van

BR Mk 2 air-braked stock
Up working: Heysham dep 06.45

The LMS concentrated Belfast traffic at Heysham from the late 1920s, and the 'Ulster Express' was reassigned from Fleetwood. Modern stock was provided for the service, the 1934 formation shown consisting primarily of Period 3 coaches. One of the 10-seat Lounge Brake Firsts built in 1928 was also included in the set. A Kitchen Car with partner open vehicles were initially used for the train but by 1934 had been replaced by a new Restaurant First and a 60ft Period 2 Open Third. Two Brake Composites for Colne and Rochdale respectively, were carried as far as Crewe. A Scenery Van for Holyhead was also detached at Crewe; a similar vehicle was on the up train from Heysham. The grouping of the Third Class coaches ahead of the dining vehicles, with the First Class accommodation (in Composites) at the rear corresponded closely to current BR practice. The postwar train was considerably larger but the general formation remained the same. A three-car dining set, including a Kitchen Car, was used in the postwar train. The Open First regularly assigned to this set was No 7555 which had been modified internally in 1947 with loose chairs. By 1954 the train had been reduced to nine vehicles, most of the set now being BR standard coaches. The formation remained much the same during the next 10 years, the the LMS Kitchen Car being replaced by a BR Kitchen Buffet in the early 1960s. The service continued to operate after the Euston electrification and for a time was formed out of the 10.00 Glasgow-Euston set. It had returned to an out-and-home working for a Mk 2 air-braked set when it ceased to operate in April 1975 with the withdrawal of the Heysham-Belfast shipping service.

Above:
The down day 'Irish Mail' at Chester in about 1930 headed by 'Royal Scot' 4-6-0 No 6146 *The Rifle Brigade*. Apart from the LMS Brake Van, the leading vehicles were pre-grouping. More modern stock, in the form of a Kitchen Car and partner Open coaches, was further back in the train. *Real Photographs T8392*

20.50 Euston-Holyhead (The 'Irish Mail')

1923
Euston dep 20.50

BV	BV	PS	PS	BV	S1	S1	BV	B3	CC	CC	B3	CC	CC	BV

Brake Van 50ft
Brake Van 50ft or 57ft
PO Sorting Van 50ft
PO Sorting Van 50ft
Brake Van 50ft
Sleeper First 65ft
Sleeper First 65ft
Brake Van 50ft
Corr Brake Third 57ft
Corr Composite 57ft
Corr Composite 57ft
Corr Brake Third 57ft
Corr Composite 57ft
Corr Composite 57ft
Brake Van 50ft

LNWR stock
Up working: Holyhead dep 00.13

1934
Euston dep 20.50

PV	PS	PS	S1	S3	B3	CC	CC	B3	C3	BV	BV	BV

PO Van 50ft or 57ft
PO Sorting Van 50ft
PO Sorting Van 60ft
Sleeper First 65ft
Sleeper Third 60ft
Corr Brake Third (24)
Corr Composite (18/24)
Corr Composite (18/24)
Corr Brake Third (24)
Corr Third (42)
Brake Van
Brake Van
Brake Van Birkenhead

Up working: Holyhead dep 00.13

1949
Euston dep 20.45

BV	S3	S1	C3	C3	O3	O3	O3	O1	C1	B1	BV	BV	BV	BV

Brake Van Steel
Sleeper Third
Sleeper First
Corr Third (42)
Corr Third (42)
Open Third (56)
Open Third (56)
Open Third (56)
Open First (42)
Corr First (33)
Corr Brake First
Brake Van Birkenhead
Brake Van Liverpool
Brake Van Manchester LR
Brake Van Manchester V

LMS stock
Up working: Holyhead dep 01.00

1954
Euston dep 20.45

BV	S3	S1	C3	B3	CC	C3	C3	C3	C3	R3	B3

Brake Van Steel (LMS)
Sleeper Third (LMS)
Sleeper First (LMS)
Corr Third (42) (LMS)
Corr Brake Third (BR1)
Corr Composite (BR1)
Corr Third (BR1)
Corr Third (BR1)
Corr Third (BR1)
Corr Third (BR1)
Restaurant Third (30) (LMS)
Corr Brake Third (24) (LMS)

Up working: Holyhead dep 01.10

1963

Euston dep 20.42

BV	S2	S1	C1	B2	C2	R2	C2	C2	C2	C2	B2

Brake Van
Sleeper Second (BR1)
Sleeper First (LMS)
Corr First (BR1)
Corr Brake Second (BR1)
Corr Second (BR1)
Restaurant Second (30) (LMS)
Corr Second (BR1)
Corr Second (BR1)
Corr Second (BR1)
Corr Second (BR1)
Corr Brake Second (24) (LM)

Up working: Holyhead dep 01.10

1973

Euston dep 20.55

BV	BV	SC	O2	O2	O2	O2	O2	RB	O1	C1	B1

Brake Van
Brake Van
Sleeper Composite
Tourist Open Second
Tourist Open Second
Tourist Open Second
Tourist Open Second
Tourist Open Second
Restaurant Buffet (12)
Open First
Corr First
Corr Brake First

BR dual heated 100mph stock
Up working: Holyhead dep 08.45 (except Sleeping Car dep 01.10)

1983

Euston dep 21.45

B2	O2	O2	O2	O2	O2	RB	O1	O1	O1	BV	BV

Open Brake Second
Tourist Open Second
Tourist Open Second
Tourist Open Second
Tourist Open Second
Tourist Open Second
Restaurant Buffet (18)
Open First
Open First
Open First
Brake Van
Brake Van

Mk 2 air-conditioned stock
Up working: Holyhead dep 05.22

The evening 'Irish Mail' was one of the LNWR's oldest established trains, and was already carrying a Sleeping Car in the 1880s. In fact, there was some similarity between the 1910 formation and that shown for 1923. One of the new four-berth Sleeping Cars went into the set at the beginning of the 1928 winter timetable.

Period 3 compartment stock was used for the 1934 train but the Sleeper First and probably the Post Office Vans were built by the LNWR. A few changes occurred during the next four years. A Corridor First and Corridor Third replaced the two Corridor Composites and another Corridor Third was added. Also one of the new 65ft Sleeper Thirds replaced the older car. The TPO portion was discontinued in August 1940. It did not reappear after the war so the number of passenger coaches was increased. A Restaurant Third went into the formation in 1951 but was only used to serve light refreshments. A pair of Sleepers continued to run in the train after nationalisation, the Sleeper Third remaining as a four-berth type until replaced by a BR standard Sleeper in 1958. LMS stock was still included in the formation well into the 1960s, but 10 years later BR Mk 2 stock was employed. The Sleeping Car service was withdrawn as from 1983, a Sleeper Composite having been used for at least 10 years. It was reinstated in 1985, but only in the up direction, an SLEP being worked down empty on the 17.03 from Euston.

Left:
The two day 'Irish Mail' trains passing near Colwyn Bay. Their basic formation in 1934 was: BV, PS, B3, CC, O3, O3, KC, 01, CC, CC, B3, CC. A Post Office Van was not carried after the war.
W. Rear collection

Below:
Rebuilt 'Scot' No 46156 *The South Wales Borderer* leads the up 'Irish Mail' past Hillmorton, south of Rugby, in the spring of 1954.
Derek Smith

Left:
During the 1950s the 17.15 Euston-Holyhead 'Emerald Isle Express' was regularly loaded to as many as 15 vehicles out of Euston. It is shown here leaving Watford on 1 August 1955 behind rebuilt No 46100 *Royal Scot* with a mix of LMS (Period 3) and BR standard stock. The specified formation in the previous year had been: B3, 2×C3, CC, C1, R1, O3, BV (Holyhead), B3, CC (Birkenhead), B3, C3, CC, B3, BV (Llandudno). However, the train shown did not correspond exactly with this. *A. R. Carpenter*

23.05 Euston-Dundee/Perth

1926

Euston dep 23.05

BC	S1	CC	BV	SC	BC	S1	S1	B3	C3

Vehicle	Destination
Corr Brake Composite 57ft	Dundee
Sleeper First 65ft	Dundee
Corr Composite 57ft	Aberdeen
Brake Van 50ft	Aberdeen
Composite Sleeper (FO) — Oban	
Corr Brake Composite 57ft	Edinburgh
Sleeper First 68ft	Edinburgh
Sleeper First 68ft	Edinburgh
Corr Brake Third 57ft	Edinburgh
Corr Third 57ft (FO)	Edinburgh

Up working: Dundee dep 21.20

1934

Euston dep 22.50

BV	CC	BV	S3	S1	BC	S1	S3	CC	B3	PS	PS

Vehicle	Destination
Brake Van Steel	Aberdeen
Corr Composite (18/24)	Aberdeen
Brake Van — Perth	
Sleeper Third 65ft	Dundee
Sleeper First 65ft	Dundee
Corr Brake Composite (9/21)	Dundee
Sleeper First 68ft	Edinburgh
Sleeper Third 65ft	Edinburgh
Corr Composite (18/24)	Edinburgh
Corr Brake Third (24)	Edinburgh
PO Sorting Van 57ft	Carlisle
PO Sorting Van 60ft	Carlisle

Up working: Dundee dep 21.20

1949

Euston dep 22.50

BV	S1	S3	C3	C3	CC	B3	O3	CC	B3	BV	PS	PS	PS	PS

Vehicle	Destination
Brake Van	Perth
Sleeper First	Perth
Sleeper Third	Perth
Corr Third (42) (FO)	Perth
Corr Third (42) (FO)	Perth
Corr Composite (18/24)	Perth
Corr Brake Third (24)	Perth
Open Third (56)	Carlisle
Corr Composite (18/24)	Carlisle
Corr Brake Third (24)	Carlisle
Brake Van	Carlisle
PO Sorting Van 60ft	Carlisle
PO Sorting Van 60ft	Carlisle
PO Sorting Van 60ft (FO)	Carlisle
PO Sorting Van 60ft (FX) — Crewe	

LMS stock

Up working: Perth dep 20.15

1954

Euston dep 22.52

BV	BV	S1	S3	C3	C3	C3	CC	B3	PS	PS	PT	PS

Vehicle	Destination
Brake Van Steel	Perth
Brake Van	Perth
Sleeper First	Perth
Sleeper Third (2 Berth)	Perth
Corr Third (42) (FO)	Perth
Corr Third (42) (FO)	Perth
Corr Third (42) (FO)	Perth
Corr Composite (18/24)	Perth
Corr Brake Third (24)	Perth
PO Sorting Van 60ft	Carlisle
PO Sorting Van 60ft	Carlisle
PO Tender Van 50ft	Carlisle
PO Sorting Van 60ft — Crewe	

LMS stock

Up working: Perth dep 21.00

1965

Euston dep 22.50

BV	BV	S1	S2	CC	B2	BV	PT	PS	PS

Brake Van (FX)
Brake Van (FX)
Sleeper First
Sleeper Second
Corr Composite
Corr Brake Second
Brake Van
PO Tender Van 50ft
PO Sorting Van 60ft
PO Sorting Van 60ft

BR Mk 1 stock
Up working: Perth dep 21.00

1973

Euston dep 22.30

BV	B2	C2	C2	C2	CC	SC	SC	S2	S1	SC	BV	BV

Brake Van
Corr Brake Second
Corr Second
Corr Second
Corr Second
Corr Composite
Sleeper Composite
Sleeper Composite
Sleeper Second
Sleeper First
Sleeper Composite (FO)
Brake Van
Brake Van — Crewe

BR dual heated stock
Up working: Perth dep 22.25

1983

Euston dep 22.40

UV	UV	SP	SE	SP	SE	SP	SE	SP	SE	O2	BV	BV

General Utility Van (Motorail) } Stirling
General Utility Van (Motorail) }
Sleeper (Pantry) } Perth
Sleeper }
Sleeper (Pantry) }
Sleeper }
Sleeper (Pantry) } Glasgow
Sleeper }
Sleeper (Pantry) }
Sleeper }
Tourist Open Second }
Brake Van }
Brake Van — Crewe

BR Mk 3 stock
Up working: Perth dep 22.25

This train was divided more than once on its journey north in 1926. Edinburgh coaches were detached at Carstairs where a Pullman car was inserted between the Dundee and Aberdeen portions to provide breakfast. One of the Pullmans originally supplied to the Caledonian, *Mary Beaton*, was assigned around this time. Sleeping Cars were carried to Edinburgh and Dundee (the Sleepers for Aberdeen had left on the 19.30 from Euston). The 68ft Sleepers in the Edinburgh portion could have been of WCJS or LMS origin but the Dundee car was of pre-grouping origin. On Friday nights a WCJS Composite Sleeper (one of the unusual dual-width type) was dropped at Stirling for Oban. At Perth, the Aberdeen portion went forward with the 07.00 from Glasgow which consisted of a Brake Composite, Pullman car (*Bonnie Jean* in 1927) and a Brake Third. The Brake Composites from London to Edinburgh and Dundee were specified as end brake vehicles with 12/24 seating, indicating they were WCJS toplight type to Diagram 39. Starting with the winter 1928 timetable a Sleeper Third was added to both the Edinburgh and Dundee portions.

The formation shown for 1934 is representative of that used during the 1930s, provided allowance is made for the progressive updating of vehicles. For example, the First Class Sleepers were replaced soon afterwards by new cars. All the compartment stock was of Period 3 design by 1934. A Pullman car, now owned by the LMS, was still attached at Carstairs at this time but was changed to a conventional Restaurant Car in the following year. The Post Office Vans at the rear constituted the North Western Down Night TPO. The two Carlisle vans were sent empty later to Glasgow to go into the Up Special TPO.

At the start of the British Railways era the train terminated at Perth. The Edinburgh portion had been eliminated, as had the Restaurant Car from Carstairs. A Sleeper First and a Sleeper Third remained but worked to Perth instead of Dundee, the Sleeper Third being replaced by a new two-berth car in the early 1950s. There was little change during the subsequent decade; the train was still formed primarily from LMS stock in 1963, only the Sleeper Second being a BR standard. The North Western TPO eventually became a separate mail train, allowing the number of Sleeping Cars to be increased. The formation remained fairly constant during the 1970s. Four Sleeper Seconds were added in 1982 for Motorail passengers to Stirling who had previously travelled from Kensington. However, the following year the train changed over to Mk 3 stock and commenced operation as a combined train for Glasgow and Perth.

Top:
BR 'Clan' Pacific No 72008 *Clan MacLeod* prepares to leave Stirling with a Perth-Euston train on 1 March 1963. *Rev R. T. Hughes*

Above:
'Duchess' Pacific No 46235 *City of Birmingham* heads a Perth-London train near Auchterrader in July 1958. Note the variety of stock.
W. J. V. Anderson

23.45 Euston-Glasgow (The 'Night Scot'/'Night Limited')

1923

Euston dep 23.45

B3	CC	S1	S1	S1	PK	C3	BV

Corr Brake Third 57ft (WCJS)
Corr Composite 50ft (WCJS)
Sleeper First 65ft
Sleeper First 68ft (WCJS)
Sleeper First 68ft (WCJS)
Pullman Car (ex-Carlisle)
Corr Third 57ft (WCJS)
Brake Van 50ft (WCJS)

Up working: Glasgow dep 22.30

1926

Euston dep 23.45

BV	CC	S1	S1	S1	S1	PC	CC	C3	C3	BV

Brake Van 50ft } St Enoch
Corr Composite 57ft } St Enoch
Sleeper First 65ft } St Enoch
Sleeper First 68ft
Sleeper First 68ft
Sleeper First 68ft
Pullman Car (ex-Carlisle)
Corr Composite 57ft
Corr Third 57ft
Corr Third 57ft
Brake Van 50ft

Up working: Glasgow dep 22.30

1938

Euston dep 23.45

BV	S1	S1	S1	R1	OC	S3	S3	CC	C3	C3	C3	BV

Brake Van Steel
Sleeper First 69ft
Sleeper First 69ft
Sleeper First 69ft
Restaurant First (24) (Carlisle)
Open Composite (18/18)
Sleeper Third 65ft
Sleeper Third 65ft
Corr Composite (18/24)
Corr Third (42)
Corr Third (42)
Corr Third (42) (FO)
Brake Van Steel

Up working: Glasgow dep 22.45

1949

Euston dep 23.40

BV	S1	S1	S1	S1	S1	R1	OC	S3	S3	CC	CC	C3	C3	C3	BV

Brake Van Steel
Sleeper First
Sleeper First
Sleeper First
Sleeper First
Sleeper First
Restaurant First (24) } (ex-Carlisle)
Open Composite (18/18) } (ex-Carlisle)
Sleeper Third
Sleeper Third
Corr Composite (18/24)
Corr Composite (18/24)
Corr Third 42
Corr Third 42
Corr Third 42
Brake Van

Up working: Glasgow dep 22.10

1954

Euston dep 23.50

BV	S1	S1	S1	S1	S1	S1	S1	S3	S3	S3	S3	BV

Brake Van Steel
Sleeper First
Sleeper First
Sleeper First
Sleeper First
Sleeper First
Sleeper First
Sleeper First
Sleeper Third
Sleeper Third
Sleeper Third
Sleeper Third
Brake Van

Up working: Glasgow dep 22.20

1965

Euston dep 21.50

BV	S1	S1	S1	S1	PC	S1	S1	S1	S1	BV

Brake Van
Sleeper First (Carlisle)
Sleeper First
Sleeper First
Sleeper First
Pullman
Sleeper First
Sleeper First
Sleeper First
Sleeper First
Brake Van

BR Mk 1 stock
Up working: Glasgow dep 22.45

1975

Euston dep 23.00

BV	S2	S1	S2	S1	S1	S1	PC	S1	S1	S1	S1	BV

Brake Van
Sleeper Second
Sleeper First
Sleeper Second
Sleeper First
Sleeper First
Sleeper First
Pullman
Sleeper First
Sleeper First
Sleeper First
Sleeper First
Brake Van

BR Mk 1 stock
Up working: Glasgow dep 23.10

1983

Euston dep 23.30

BV	SP	SP	SE	SP	SE	SP	SE	SP	SE	SP	SP	BV

Brake Van } Carlisle
Sleeper Either Class (Pantry) }
Sleeper Either Class (Pantry)
Sleeper Either Class
Sleeper Either Class (Pantry)
Sleeper Either Class
Sleeper Either Class (Pantry)
Sleeper Either Class
Sleeper Either Class (Pantry)
Sleeper Either Class
Sleeper Either Class (Pantry)
Sleeper Either Class (Pantry)
Brake Van

BR Mk 3 stock
Up working: Glasgow dep 23.15

Both the LNWR and MR had each provided a 23.45 Sleeping Car train from London to Glasgow. Restaurant Cars were attached to both at Carlisle. The LMS soon cancelled the St Pancras departure, the Euston train then going to Glasgow (St Enoch) over the G&SWR route. The train reverted to the Caledonian route in the summer of 1925 with a portion detached at Carlisle for St Enoch. The 1927 formation shows three coaches, including a Sleeping Car, travelling this way; they were worked empty to Glasgow Central for the up return. A Pullman car was added to the main portion at Carlisle. During 1927 and 1928 the assigned car was *Flora McDonald*, one of the batch of Pullmans which had gone to the Caledonian Railway in 1914. Third Class Sleepers were added to the train in 1928.

The working was altered in 1934 with the St Enoch portion leaving Euston as a separate train. The main train now contained five sleepers (arranged as shown for 1938), the two Sleeper Thirds being new 65ft vehicles to Period 3 design. The leading Sleeper First was a 65ft pre-grouping vehicle, while the other two 68ft cars could have been of LNWR or LMS types — most probably the latter in view of the status of the train. All three Sleeper Firsts were soon replaced by new 69ft stock built in 1935/36. The Restaurant Car added at Carlisle continued to be a Pullman, owned by the LMS from 1933, until replaced by a Restaurant First paired with a Composite Open in 1936.

The postwar train was much larger with seven Sleepers and five compartment coaches. Carlisle resumed the prewar two-coach addition for breakfast service. New two-berth Third Class sleepers, still very much LMS in appearance, were turned out by Wolverton in 1951/52 and one went into the formation. A new all sleeping car train was introduced between London and Glasgow in about 1953. The formation was made up of seven Firsts and four Thirds of the two-berth type. In 1966 the formation was modified to become an all First Class sleeper train and was named the 'Night Limited'. Second Class stock reappeared in 1969. A modified Pullman car, styled the *Nightcap Bar*, worked between Euston and Glasgow. Several Pullmans spent their last days on this duty including *Pegasus* (from the 'Golden Arrow'), and the modern *Hadrian Bar*. The *Nightcap Bar* lasted until the end of the 1970s. By 1981 the trains carried 13 sleepers (nine Firsts and four Seconds), two sleepers for Carlisle (First and Second) having recently been added. Mk 3 Sleeping Cars formed the summer 1983 train.

09.00 St Pancras-Edinburgh (The 'Thames-Forth/Waverley')

1927
St Pancras dep 09.00

BV	C3	OC	RC	BC	BC

Brake Van
Corr Third
Open Composite (12/35)
Restaurant Composite (12/12)
Corr Brake Composite
Corr Brake Composite — Aberdeen

Up working: Edinburgh dep 10.05

1938
St Pancras dep 09.05

BC	C3	B3	OC	R1	CC	BT	BC

Corr Brake Composite — Leeds
Corr Third (42) (FO)
Corr Brake Third (24)
Open Third (42)
Restaurant First (24)
Corr Composite (18/24)
Corr Brake Third (24)
Corr Brake Composite (9/21) — Halifax

Up working: Edinburgh dep 10.03

1949
St Pancras dep 08.55

B3	C3	C3	C3	C3	O3	R1	C1	CC	B3

Corr Brake Third (24)
Corr Third (42)
Corr Third (42)
Corr Third (42)
Corr Third (42)
Open Third (56)
Restaurant First (24)
Corr First (33)
Corr Composite (18/24)
Corr Brake Third (24)

LMS stock
Up working: Edinburgh dep 10.06

1954
St Pancras dep 09.00

B3	C3	C3	C3	C3	C3	R3	C1	CC	B3

Corr Brake Third
Corr Third (FO)
Corr Third
Corr Third
Corr Third
Corr Third
Restaurant Third (24) (LMS)
Corr First
Corr Composite
Corr Brake Third

BR Mk 1 stock
Up working: Edinburgh dep 10.05

1960
St Pancras dep 09.00

B2	O2	O2	O2	R1	C1	CC	CC	B2

Corr Brake Second
Open Second
Open Second
Open Second
Restaurant First (24) (LMS)
Corr First
Corr Composite
Corr Composite
Corr Brake Second

BR Mk 1 stock
Up working: Edinburgh dep 10.05

1965
St Pancras dep 09.15

[loco]	B2	O2	O2	O2	R1	C1	CC	CC	B2

Corr Brake Second
Open Second
Open Second
Open Second (48)
Restaurant First (24)
Corr First
Corr Composite
Corr Composite
Corr Brake Second

BR Mk 1 stock
Up working: Edinburgh dep 10.15

The morning departure from St Pancras to Edinburgh had been a feature of the Midland Railway timetable for many years. The coaches for this service were built at Derby but were jointly owned by the Midland and North British companies. The 1927 formation was still made up of this stock except for the Open Composite which was an LMS Period 1 vehicle. The Brake Composite for Aberdeen was handed over to the LNER at Edinburgh. This was a continuation of pre-grouping practice, and was discontinued soon afterwards. Another Brake Composite, for Glasgow, was attached at Nottingham and removed at Carlisle, going forward on the 10.00 from St Pancras. A similar type of coach was attached to the up train from Edinburgh, going on to Manchester from Carlisle. In 1928 the Midland and North British coaches were divided up between the LMS and LNER. The replacement stock would, most probably, have been LMS-built vehicles. The 1938 train consisted of modern vehicles, all the compartment stock being of the Period 3 style. A Brake Composite for Halifax had been added to the formation several years earlier and was transferred at Sheffield. After nationalisation the formation had grown to 10 vehicles, the additions being mostly Corridor Thirds. By 1954 there had been a changeover to new BR standard vehicles. An LMS Third Class Restaurant Car was in use at this time but as it acted as a Buffet; there was no partner Open vehicle. It had changed back to the normal dining formation by 1958. A BR standard Restaurant First replaced the LMS type in the early 1960s but otherwise there was little change to the formation during the last decade of operation.

Above:
The up 'Thames Forth Express' at Ais Gill Summit on the Settle-Carlisle line on 10 August 1949. 'Black Five' 4-6-0 No 45268 is in charge of five vehicles of LMS Period 3 design.
H. Weston

09.50 St Pancras-Glasgow (The 'Thames-Clyde Express')

1927
St Pancras dep 09.50

BV	C3	O3	O3	KC	O1	B1

Brake Van
Corr Third
Open Third
Open Third
Kitchen Car
Open First
Corr Brake First

Up working: Glasgow dep 09.15

1938
St Pancras dep 10.00

B3	C3	O3	O3	KC	OC	CC	B1

Corr Brake Third (24)
Corr Third (42)
Open Third (42)
Open Third (42)
Kitchen Car
Open Composite (18/18)
Corr Composite (18/24)
Brake First

Up working: Glasgow dep 09.35

1949
St Pancras dep 09.20

O3	B3	C3	C3	C3	C3	C3	O3	R1	C1	B1	BV

Open Third (56) (MFO)
Corr Brake Third (24)
Corr Third (42)
Corr Third (42)
Corr Third (42)
Corr Third (42)
Corr Third (42)
Open Third (56)
Restaurant First (24)
Corr First (33)
Corr Brake First (27)
Brake Van

LMS stock
Up working: Glasgow dep 09.20

1955
St Pancras dep 10.00

B3	C3	C3	C3	C3	C3	O3	R1	C1	CC	B3

Corr Third Brake
Corr Third (FO)
Corr Third
Corr Third
Corr Third
Corr Third
Open Third (56) (LMS)
Restaurant First (24) (LMS)
Corr First
Corr Composite
Corr Third Brake

BR Mk 1 Stock
Up working: Glasgow dep 09.20

1965
St Pancras dep 10.15

B2	C2	C2	O2	O2	RB	O1	C1	CC	B2

Corr Brake Second
Corr Second
Corr Second
Open Second
Open Second
Restaurant Buffet (23)
Open First
Corr First
Corr Composite
Corr Brake Second

BR Mk 1 stock
Up working: Glasgow dep 09.02

1975
St Pancras dep 08.00

B1	C1	O2	O1	RB	O2	O2	O2	B2

Corr Brake First
Corr First
Tourist Open Second
Open First
Restaurant/Buffet (23)
Tourist Open Second
Tourist Open Second
Tourist Open Second
Corr Brake Second

BR dual-heated 100mph stock
Up working: Glasgow dep 10.45

The mid-morning service to Glasgow had been one of the Midland Railway's premier trains. It seems almost certain therefore that the 1927 formation shown would have consisted of new LMS Period 1 stock. A Brake Composite was attached behind the locomotive at Carlisle, this being a through coach from Nottingham to Glasgow which had travelled north on the 09.00 from St Pancras to Edinburgh. The same coach started its return south on the up train to St Pancras along with a Brake Composite for Bristol (transferred at Sheffield). By 1938 the formation had grown and was now mainly composed of Period 3 stock. A Brake Composite (9/21) for Bristol was still carried on the up train. The postwar train provided considerably more Third Class accommodation. A Restaurant First was used for a while but there was a return to the prewar Kitchen Car arrangements in 1950. This lasted until 1955 when a First Class vehicle took over once more. Also by this time the remainder of the train had changed to BR standard stock. There was little change in the formation during the next 10 years, the LMS Restaurant Car eventually yielding to a BR standard vehicle in the early 1960s.

Starting in 1966 the St Pancras to Glasgow and Edinburgh trains were combined during the winter but continued to run independently in the summer. Improved rolling stock, made up of late Mk 1 and Mk 2 coaches cascaded from the West Coast Route, went into the train in 1973. The service from St Pancras was terminated at end of the 1975/76 timetable with Nottingham becoming the starting point. It was later replaced by the Harwich-Glasgow train.

Above:
BR standard stock, in the form of a Brake Third, had just started to go into the 'Thames-Clyde Express' when it was photographed crossing Smardale viaduct in June 1952. The remainder of the set appears to be Period 3 stock apart from the Period 1 Kitchen Car. Rebuilt 'Scot' No 46109 *Royal Engineers* is in charge.
E. D. Bruton

Left:
Rebuilt 'Royal Scot' 4-6-0 No 46108 *Seaforth Highlander* leaves Skipton North Junction with the down 'Thames-Clyde Express' on 28 June 1952.
C. Bendall

Below:
By 1955 the 'Thames-Clyde Express' consisted of BR standard stock with the exception of a Restaurant Car which had replaced the Kitchen Car. The train is shown at Kirkby Stephen in July 1957. Class 5 4-6-0 No 44958 leads 'Jubilee' No 45679 *Armada*.
P. Ransome-Wallis

14.30 St Pancras-Manchester

1938
St Pancras dep 14.30

B3	C3	O3	R1	CC	B1	BC

Corr Brake Third (24)
Corr Third (42)
Open Third (56)
Restaurant First (24)
Corr Composite (18/24)

Corr Brake First (27)
Corr Brake Composite (9/21) — Buxton

Up working: Manchester dep 07.20

1955
St Pancras dep 14.15

B3	C3	C3	CC	O1	CC	B3	BC	CA	B3

Corr Brake Third (BR1)
Corr Third (BR1)
Corr Third (BR1)
Corr Composite (BR1)
Open First (42) (LMS)
Corr Composite (BR1)

Corr Brake Third (BR1)
Corr Brake Composite (9/21) (LMS) — Buxton
Cafeteria Car } Derby
Corr Brake Third (24) (LMS) } Derby

Up working: Manchester dep 09.00

1965
St Pancras dep 14.25

CC	B3	C3	O3	C1	O1	R1	O2	C2	B2	C1

Corr Composite
Corr Brake Third
Corr Third
Open Third
Corr First
Open First
Restaurant First (24)

Open Second
Corr Second
Corr Brake Second
Corr First

BR Mk 1 stock
Up working: Manchester dep 18.55

During the 1930s the sets employed on the principal Manchester services appear to have been formed mainly from modern LMS stock. For example, the seating specification in 1938 for the 14.30 set indicates that it was almost certainly made up from Period 2 and 3 vehicles. A comparison with the other contemporary Manchester sets indicates that the 12.30 and 16.30 down trains had a Corridor Third instead of a Composite and the 10.30 carried an additional Corridor Third but otherwise they were of similar make-up to the 14.30. The through coach to Buxton, which was detached at Millers Dale, dated back to at least 1903. A Restaurant First continued to work in the train for about 10 years after the war, but was then replaced by a Cafeteria Car which came off at Derby. Several Cafeteria Cars, which were mainly conversions from Ambulance Cars (originally LMS and LNER stock), had been allocated to the Midland Division at this time. They were also employed in two other Manchester sets. However, the Cafeteria Car did not stay for long in the 14.15, being replaced in 1958 with one of the LMS-built Buffet Cars. The Brake Composite which went to Buxton was terminated in 1963. During the last few years of operation the load was increased and a Restaurant First, now a BR standard type, worked through to Manchester once again. No doubt this was part of the offload plan to relieve Euston during the electrification work. When this was completed in 1966 the London-Manchester services were transferred from St Pancras. Note that the Brakes were marshalled inside the 1965 set to avoid drawing up at some stations.

16.55 St Pancras-Bradford (The 'Yorkshireman')

1925

St Pancras 16.55

B3	O3	O3	KC	O1	O3	B3

Open Brake Third (40)
Open Third (56)
Open Third (42)
Kitchen Car
Open First (36)
Open Third (56)
Open Brake Third (40)

Up working: Bradford dep 09.10

1938

St Pancras dep 17.10

B3	C3	O3	O3	KC	O1	B1

Corr Brake Third (24)
Corr Third (42)
Open Third (56)
Open Third (42)
Kitchen Car
Open First (42)
Corr Brake First (27)

Up working: Bradford dep 09.05

1947

St Pancras dep 16.50

O3	O3	B3	C3	C3	C3	C3	C3	O3	R1	O1	B1

Open Third (56) (MFO)
Open Third (56) (MFO)
Corr Brake Third (24)
Corr Third (42)
Corr Third (42)
Corr Third (42)
Corr Third (42)
Corr Third (42)
Open Third (56)
Restaurant First (24)
Open First (42)
Corr Brake First (27)

Up working: Bradford dep 09.15

1955

St Pancras dep 16.50

C3	B3	C3	C3	O3	KC	O1	C1	C1	CC	B3	BV

Corr Third (BR1) (MFO)
Corr Brake Third (BR1)
Corr Third (BR1)
Corr Third (BR1)
Open Third (BR1)
Kitchen Car (LMS)
Open First (BR1)
Corr First (36) (LMS)
Corr First (36) (LMS)
Corr Composite (BR1)
Corr Brake Third (BR1)
Brake Van — Nottingham-Carnforth

Up working: Bradford dep 09.12

1960

St Pancras dep 17.06

O2	CC	B2	O2	R1	C1	B2	CC	B3

Open Second
Corr Composite
Corr Brake Second
Open Second
Restaurant First (24) (LMS)
Corr First
Corr Brake Second
Corr Composite } Halifax
Corr Brake Third } Halifax

BR Mk 1 NE Region stock
Up working: Bradford dep 08.52

1975

St Pancras dep 17.00

O2	O2	O2	O2	B2	RB	O1	C1	C1

Tourist Second Open
Tourist Second Open
Tourist Second Open
Tourist Second Open
Open Brake Second
Restaurant Buffet (23)
Open First
Corr First
Corr First

BR Mk 2 air-braked stock
Up working: Leeds dep 09.16

This train was introduced in March 1925, running via Royston and Thornhill to avoid Leeds. It was the first LMS train to be entirely made up of Open stock, all the vehicles in the seven-coach set being of new (Period 1) design. Meal service was offered at every seat. By the mid-1930s the two Open Brake Thirds had been replaced by a Corridor Brake, and the 1938 formation shows one Open third had been replaced by a Corridor third. After the war the train did not return. The service was now provided by the Bradford train which went via Leeds in prewar days and had carried a two-coach Heysham portion (Composite and Brake Third). A Restaurant First was employed initially but was changed to a Kitchen Car with partner Open coaches in about 1948; they continued through most of the following decade. As part of the 1948 livery experiments the train was painted chocolate and cream. The set consisted primarily of BR standard stock by 1955, including the Open First and Open Third vehicles used for dining; two Corridor Firsts and the Kitchen Car remained as LMS stock. A portion for Halifax was added in 1960 (and withdrawn from 1962), as a result of the termination of the 'South Yorkshireman' service from Marylebone. Stock was now being supplied by the NE Region, and although the Restaurant First remained an LMS type it carried an E-prefix to the number. A BR standard Restaurant/Buffet was soon brought in as a replacement. The train disappeared in 1977 after having been cut back earlier to terminate at Leeds. Latterly it was formed from air-braked Mk 2 coaches cascaded from the West Coast Main Line.

Above:
The 16.50 St Pancras-Bradford leaving St Pancras in August 1948. The set was painted in the experimental livery of chocolate and cream and the locomotive 'Jubilee' 4-6-0 No 45694 *Bellerophon* in experimental apple green livery. *E. D. Bruton*

The 'Midland Pullman'

1960
St Pancras dep 18.10

MB	MK	TP	TP	MK	MB

Motor Brake First
Motor Kitchen First
Trailer Parlour First
Trailer Parlour First
Motor Kitchen First
Motor Brake First

Up working: Manchester dep 08.50

The only diesel-electric Pullman car train to work on British Railways went into service between St Pancras and Manchester (Central) in July 1960 as the 'Midland Pullman'. Two First Class only six-car sets, one acting as spare, were supplied by Metropolitan-Cammell to the LM Region. The 12 cars consisted of four 12-seat Motor Brake Firsts (M60090-3), four 18-seat Motor Kitchen Firsts (M60730-3), and four 36-seat Trailer Parlour Firsts (M60740-3). During the first week of operation the set was formed from M60092, M60732, M60742, M60743, M60733, M60093. There was a round trip from London to Leicester during the day, and from October 1961 this was extended to Nottingham. To accommodate this extension the departure time from Manchester was put back to 07.45. Following the concentration of London-Manchester services on Euston in 1966 the two sets were transferred to the Western Region, where similar services on the routes from Paddington to Bristol and Birmingham had been introduced in September 1960 with eight-car sets of a different layout.

Above:
Principal London-Manchester services were transferred to the Midland line while electrification was being extended into Euston. A train of six Metro-Cammell air-conditioned Pullmans, two of them power cars, was built to provide a service between the two cities in 3hr 10min — the fastest scheduled up to the introduction of the new train in 1960. The first class only 'Midland Pullman', in blue livery instead of the traditional Pullman brown and cream, climbs towards Chinley South Junction in the early stages of the up journey.
John Clarke

21.15 St Pancras-Edinburgh

1927

St Pancras dep 21.15

BV	C3	S1	C3	CC	BV

Brake Van	Perth
Corr Third Sleeper First Corr Third	Edinburgh
Corr Composite Brake Van	Aberdeen

M&NB stock
Up working: Edinburgh dep 21.55

1938

St Pancras dep 21.15

BV	C3	SC	CC	BV

Brake Van (LMS or LNER)
Corr Third (LMS or LNER)
Sleeper Composite (LMS or LNER)
Corr Composite (18/24)
Brake Van

Up working: Edinburgh dep 21.55

1949

St Pancras dep 21.00

BV	SC	CC	CC	C3	C3	C3	O3	O3	BV

Brake Van
Sleeper Composite
Corr Composite (18/24)
Corr Composite (18/24)
Corr Third (42)
Corr Third (42)
Corr Third (42)
Open Third (56) (FO)
Open Third (FO)
Brake Van

LMS stock
Up working: Edinburgh dep 21.53

1955

St Pancras dep 21.05

BV	SC	SC	S3	S1	CC	CC	C3	C3	C3	BV

Brake Van
Sleeper Composite
Sleeper Composite
Sleeper Third
Sleeper First
Corr Composite (18/24)
Corr Composite (18/24)
Corr Third (42)
Corr Third (42)
Corr Third (42)
Brake Van

LMS stock
Up working: Edinburgh dep 21.53

1963

St Pancras dep 21.20

BV	S2	S1	CC	CC	C2	C2	C2	BV

Brake Van
Sleeper Second
Sleeper First
Corr Composite
Corr Composite
Corr Second
Corr Second
Corr Second
Brake Van

BR Mk 1 stock
Up working: Edinburgh dep 22.05

Prior to grouping, this service was operated with Midland & North British Joint Stock. Included in this fleet of Midland-built clerestory vehicles were three Sleeper Firsts and four Sleeper Composites for the night service. For most of the year the formation was five M&NB vehicles which, from Edinburgh, were: Third, Sleeper, two Brake Composites and a Van, with an M&NB van for Manchester leading. During the peak summer season the load was increased. In 1914, for example, there were through coaches from Inverness (Sleeper Composite), Perth (Corridor Brake Composite), Aberdeen (Sleeper Composite, and Corridor Brake Third), and Fort William (Corridor Composite).

This service continued to be operated with Joint Stock for several years after grouping. Thus, the formation shown for 1927 was similar to that of a decade earlier.

Two new 65ft Sleeper Firsts were built for the M&NB by the LMS in 1927. When the Joint Stock was distributed between the two parent companies in 1928, one new Sleeper was assigned to the LNER; it remained in the St Pancras service. Of the three older Sleepers which went to the LNER, the First Class vehicle was rebuilt as Full Brake Van, and the two Composites as Brake Thirds.

The LNER built a new Sleeper Composite for the train in 1931. It was of Gresley design and was numbered 32322 in the LNER Southern Scottish Area series. Arrival of this car allowed the 65ft Sleeper built in 1927 to be sold to the LMS. Thus the formation shown for 1938 shows a Sleeper Composite, supplied alternately by the LMS and LNER. There was a similar arrangement for other vehicles but the Composite Corridor and a Brake Van appear to have been a continuous LMS responsibility.

After the war a Sleeper Composite was still rostered but the size of the regular formation had grown to eight vehicles. In 1950 the number of Sleepers was increased to two, worked by ER and LMR cars on alternate days. There seems to be little doubt that one was the former No 32322 now renumbered to 1100 in the LNER East Coast series; the other car was possibly No 1097. Within five years a Sleeper First and Sleeper Third had been added to the train, also supplied alternately by the two regions. By 1960 the two Sleeper Composites were no longer diagrammed, the whole train now consisting of BR standard stock allocated to LM Region. There were no major changes until the train ceased to run with the closure of the Waverley route.

Above:
The St Pancras-Edinburgh sleeper climbs past Bowland towards Falahill on the Waverley Route behind Gresley 'A3' Pacific No 60096 *Papyrus* on the morning of 5 August 1951.
A. C. Cawston

21.30 St Pancras-Glasgow

1927
St Pancras dep 21.30

UV	BV	BV	BV	CC	S1	S1	C3	B3

Parcels Van — Kilmarnock
Brake Van
Brake Van
Brake Van
Corr Composite
Sleeper First
Sleeper First
Corr Third
Corr Brake Third

Up working: Glasgow dep 21.15

1938
St Pancras dep 21.30

MO	BV	BV	CC	S1	S3	C3	C3	C3	BV	BV	UV

Motor Car Van 4- or 6-wheel — Carlisle
Brake Van — Kilmarnock
Brake Van
Corr Composite (18/24)
Sleeper First
Sleeper Third
Corr Third (42)
Corr Third (42) (FO)
Corr Third (42) (FO)
Brake Van
Brake Van — Leeds
Parcels Van — Bradford

Up working: Glasgow dep 21.15

1949
St Pancras dep 21.10

BV	BV	B3	C3	C3	C3	S3	S1	S1	CC	CC	BV

Brake Van — Kilmarnock
Brake Van
Corr Brake Third (42)
Corr Third (42) (FO)
Corr Third (42)
Corr Third (42)
Sleeper Third
Sleeper First
Sleeper First
Corr Composite (18/24)
Corr Composite (18/24)
Brake Van

Up working: Glasgow dep 21.05

1955
St Pancras dep 21.15

BV	BV	B3	C3	C3	C3	S3	S1	S1	CC	BV

Brake Van (LMS) — Kilmarnock
Brake Van (BR1)
Corr Brake Third (BR1)
Corr Third (BR1)
Corr Third (BR1)
Corr Third (BR1)
Sleeper Third (LMS)
Sleeper First (LMS)
Sleeper First (LMS)
Corr Composite (BR1)
Brake Van (BR1)

Up working: Glasgow dep 21.05

1965
St Pancras dep 21.30

BV	BV	B2	C2	C2	C2	CC	S2	S1	S1	BV

Brake Van — Kilmarnock
Brake Van
Corr Brake Second
Corr Second
Corr Second
Corr Second
Corr Composite
Sleeper Second
Sleeper First
Sleeper First
Brake Van

BR Mk 1 stock
Up working: Glasgow dep 21.25

1975

St Pancras dep 21.30

C2	C2	SC	S2	C2	B2	C2	C2	CC	BV	BV

Corr Second†
Corr Second†
Sleeper Composite*
Sleeper Second*
Corr Second
Corr Brake Second
Corr Second
Corr Second
Corr Composite
Brake Van
Brake Van — Leeds

* Attached at Nottingham
† Detached at Nottingham
BR dual-heated stock
Up working: Glasgow dep 22.50

Pullman Sleepers had been originally used by the Midland Railway on this Anglo-Scottish service. They were later taken into Midland stock. Between 1900 and 1911, 19 First Class Sleepers (not including four for the M&NB) were turned out by Derby. The LMS, when formed, would have continued to use these cars on the Glasgow service. By 1927, however, the LMS had constructed 30 new Sleepers and it seems probable they would have been represented in the formation shown. A Sleeper Third went into the train in the following year, apparently replacing a Sleeper First. The 1938 train consisted of modern stock including the Sleeper First and Sleeper Third carried. A regular feature of the prewar working was that a Brake Composite and Full Brake from Bristol were attached to the front of the train at Carlisle. They did not return south on the balancing up train for St Pancras but instead left on the 17.30 from Glasgow. Transit of a Motor Car Van between London and Carlisle in 1938 is of interest; the LMS owned 200 of these vehicles at this time.

Both the seating and Sleeper accommodation were greater in the postwar period as can be seen from the 1949 formation. One of the new LMS design Sleeper Thirds, with two berths in each compartment, built in 1951/52, soon replaced the prewar four-berth car. A new Sleeper service between Leeds and St Pancras was started in the early 1950s. A Sleeper Composite inaugurated the service but was soon replaced by a Sleeper First and a Sleeper Third (four-berth type). They were attached to the front of the up train from Glasgow at Leeds but returned north on the midnight train from St Pancras. In 1955 all coaches, apart from the Sleepers, were changed over to BR standard types. Although many new Mk 1 Sleepers were delivered to the LMR in 1957/58 they were not assigned to this working until about five years later. Apart from this change the 1965 formation was very similar to that of 10 years earlier. The Sleepers from Leeds travelled via the East Coast route from 1968. Between 1969 and 1972 the train ran to and from Euston. Commencing with the 1972/73 timetable the Sleepers only ran between Nottingham and Glasgow, a Composite and a First being employed. The train was withdrawn in 1977.

06.50 Barrow/Morecambe-Manchester

1926
Barrow dep 06.50

UN	**UN**	**UN**	**BC**	**BC**	**BC**

Non-Corr 3-set — Lancaster
Corr Composite Brake 54ft } Manchester
Corr Composite Brake 54ft } Manchester
Corr Composite Brake 54ft — Leeds

Down working: Manchester dep 14.10

1934
Barrow dep 07.10

UN	**UN**	**UN**	**UN**	**C3**	**CC**	**B3**	**C3**	**CC**	**B3**

Corr 4-set
Corr Third (64)
Corr Composite (18/32)
Corr Brake Third (40)
} Manchester

Corr Third (64)
Corr Composite (18/32)
Corr Brake Third (40)
} Leeds

Down working: Manchester dep 09.40

1939
Barrow dep 07.10

B3	**C3**	**CC**	**CC**	**C3**	**B3**	**BC**

Corr Brake Third (24)
Corr Third (42)
Corr Composite (18/24)
Corr Composite (18/24)
Corr Third (42)
Corr Brake Third (24)
} Manchester

Corr Brake Composite — Leeds

Down working: Manchester dep 16.10

1949
Barrow dep 06.58

B3	**CC**	**CC**	**CC**	**CC**	**B3**	**B3**	**CC**	**O3**

Corr Brake Third (24)
Corr Composite (18/24)
Corr Composite (18/24)
Corr Composite (18/24)
Corr Composite (18/24)
Corr Brake Third (24)

Corr Brake Third (24)
Corr Composite (18/24)
Open Third (56)
} (ex-Morecambe)

LMS stock
Down working: Manchester dep 15.55

1954
Barrow dep 06.58

B3	**CC**	**CC**	**C3**	**B3**	**B3**	**CC**	**C3**	**B3**	**BV**

Corr Brake Third (24)
Corr Composite (18/24)
Corr Composite (18/24)
Corr Third (42)
Corr Brake Third (24)

Corr Brake Third (24)
Corr Composite (18/24)
Corr Third (42)
Corr Brake Third (24)
Brake Van (MX)
} (ex-Morecambe)

LMS stock
Down working: Manchester dep 15.55

1965
Barrow dep 07.00

	B2	CC	B2	B2	CC	C2	C2	B2	BV

Corr Brake Second
Corr Composite
Corr Brake Second (24) (LMS)
Corr Brake Second
Corr Composite
Corr Second
Corr Second
Corr Brake Second
Brake Van (MX)
(ex-Morecambe)

BR Mk 1 stock
Up working: Manchester dep 16.03

In prewar days, the Barrow-Manchester train carried a portion for Leeds, which was dropped at Carnforth. Through coaches from Morecambe to Manchester were picked up at Lancaster. The Brake Composite for Leeds in the 1926 formation was a 54ft-long 8ft-wide vehicle, built by the Furness Railway, seating nine First and 21 Third Class passengers. The other two Brake Composites from Barrow were L&Y vehicles based at Manchester. They too were 54ft long but their width was 9ft and they had 12/32 seating. Some of the other duties for this type of L&Y vehicle in 1926 were Manchester to Morecambe and Windermere services and those from Liverpool to Whitehaven and Windermere. At Lancaster these two coaches for Manchester were attached at the rear of a four-coach Non-Corridor inter-district set which had left Morecambe at 08.15.

The working was similar in 1934 but there had been some stock changes. The four-coach set from Barrow to Manchester was described in the Carriage Working book as 'narrow stock', several such sets being based at Barrow. While Furness Railway vehicles would be expected to be represented in these sets, some LNWR and MR clerestory coaches had moved to the area by this time, so could have been included. At Lancaster the three-coach inter-corridor set forming the 08.15 Morecambe-Manchester was attached ahead of the seven coaches from Barrow. By the end of the 1930s the Barrow-Manchester stock had been upgraded, modern LMS vehicles being specified. The portion from Morecambe remained a three-coach inter-corridor set.

The train was continued after nationalisation but the through portion for Leeds was dropped. The Barrow portion had grown in size, initially being formed from some of the stock from the previous day's 12.05 from Euston. During the 1950s the Morecambe section grew in size so that by 1965 it was the larger component of the set which, by this time, was mainly comprised of BR standard stock. This through service was eliminated soon afterwards.

Above:
Stanier 'Black Five' 4-6-0 No 45383 and Fairburn Class 4MT 2-6-4T No 42119 halt at Barrow-in-Furness with a Whitehaven-Manchester Victoria train on 19 August 1960.
R. J. Farrell

08.05 Birmingham-Newcastle

1949
Birmingham dep 08.05

B3	C3	CC	CC	C3	B3	R3	OC

Corr Brake Third (24)
Corr Third (42)
Corr Composite (18/24)
Corr Composite (18/24)
Corr Third (42)
Corr Brake Third (24)
Restaurant Third (30)
Open Composite (18/18) } (ex-Derby)

LMS stock
Up working: Newcastle dep 16.05

1954
Birmingham dep 08.02

B3	C3	CC	CC	C3	B3	BU	B3

Corr Brake Third (24)
Corr Third (42)
Corr Composite (18/24)
Corr Composite (18/24)
Corr Third (42)
Corr Brake Third (24)
Buffet Car (24) (LNER)
Open Brake Third (48) (LNER) } (ex-York)

LMS stock
Up working: Newcastle dep 15.57

1960
Birmingham dep 08.05

B2	C2	CC	CC	BU	C2	C2	B2

Corr Brake Second
Corr Second
Corr Composite
Corr Composite
Miniature Buffet
Corr Second
Corr Second
Corr Brake Second

BR Mk 1 stock
Up working: Newcastle dep 15.50

1975
Birmingham dep 07.30

B2	BU	C2	C1	C2	C2	C2	C2	BV

Corr Brake Second
Miniature Buffet
Corr Second
Corr First
Corr Second
Corr Second
Corr Second
Corr Second
Brake Van

BR dual-heated 100mph stock
Up working: Newcastle dep 14.00 to Bristol

1981
Birmingham dep 07.30

BU	O2	O2	C1	O2	O2	O2	BV

Miniature Buffet
Tourist Open Second
Tourist Open Second
Corr First
Tourist Open Second
Tourist Open Second
Tourist Open Second
Brake Van

BR Mk 2 air-braked stock
Up working: Newcastle dep 13.44 to Swansea

This train was introduced in the postwar period to provide a morning service from the Midlands to Yorkshire and Tyneside. The LMS Region was always responsible for the stock and apart from the refreshment vehicle the same basic formation was maintained for many years. Initially there was no catering but in 1949 a Restaurant Third and a partner Open Composite worked between Derby and Newcastle. This was changed in the following year, an LNER Buffet and Open Brake Third being attached to the rear at York. Actually the Buffet normally employed was one of several NER Open Thirds which had been converted to Buffets during the early 1930s. It remained until 1958 when a BR standard Miniature Buffet began to work through from Birmingham. The rest of the set was changed over to BR standard stock at about the same time. By 1963 a Brake Van had replaced the leading Brake Third and the carriage working had become more complex. The set worked from Newcastle to Bristol on the return journey to form the next day's 07.40 Bristol-Bradford and then returned to Birmingham. Twelve years later the second day's working had changed to a Bristol (dep 11.36) to Manchester working: the Miniature Buffet and adjacent Brake Second only worked between Birmingham and Newcastle. The last full year of operation of the Birmingham-Newcastle train was 1981 when it consisted of Mk 2 air-braked stock which went to Swansea on the up return and formed the 07.28 Swansea-Leeds. The Miniature Buffet still came off at Birmingham. The service was replaced in 1982 by the 06.03 IC125 service from Bristol to Newcastle.

Above:
The Birmingham-Newcastle set which left at 08.05 is shown returning south in the mid-1950s. Period 3 stock was employed from Birmingham but the two LNER coaches at the front worked between York and Newcastle. The trailing vehicle of this pair was an NER Open Third converted to a Buffet Car. The locomotive is Gresley 'A3' Pacific No 60088 *Book Law*. *Ian Allan Library*

20.35 Carlisle-Perth

1927

Carlisle dep 20.35

B3	CC	RC	CC	B3	BC	BC	BV	PS

Corr Brake Third
Corr Composite } Liverpool-Glasgow
Restaurant Composite
Corr Composite } Manchester-Glasgow
Corr Brake Third
Corr Brake Composite — Manchester-Edinburgh

Corr Brake Composite } Euston-Aberdeen
Brake Van
PO Sorting Van — Carlisle-Perth

Up working: Perth dep 20.15

1938

Carlisle dep 20.22

BC	RC	O3	B3	BV	BV	PS

Corr Brake Composite 60ft
Restaurant Composite (15/21) } Manchester-Glasgow
Open Third (56)
Corr Brake Third (24)
Brake Van — Liverpool-Glasgow

Brake Van — Manchester-Glasgow
PO Sorting Van — Carlisle-Perth

Up working: Perth dep 20.15

1949

Carlisle dep 20.22

PS	B3	CC	C3

PO Sorting Van — Carlisle-Perth
Corr Brake Third (24)
Corr Composite (18/24) } Liverpool-Edinburgh
Corr Third (42)

Up working: Perth dep 20.15

1954

Carlisle dep 20.30

BV	CC	B3	BV	PS	BV

Brake Van (WO) — Burscough Bridge-Perth
Corr Composite (18/24) } Carlisle-Perth
Corr Brake Third (24)
Brake Van — Crewe-Perth

PO Sorting Van } Carlisle-Perth
Brake Van

Up working: Perth dep 20.20

1964

Carlisle dep 20.27

PS	B2	O2	O2	KB	O1	O1	C1	B1

PO Sorting Van — Carlisle-Perth
Corr Brake Second
Open Second
Open Second
Kitchen Buffet } Euston-Perth
Open First
Open First
Corr First
Corr First Brake

BR Mk 1 stock
Up working: Perth dep 20.15

1973
Carlisle dep 20.33

BV	PS	O2	B1

Brake Van
PO Sorting Van
Tourist Open Second
Corr Brake First

BR dual-heated 100mph stock
Up working: Perth dep 20.25

1983
Carlisle dep 20.50

B2	CC	PS	BV

Corr Brake Second
Corr Composite
PO Sorting Van
Brake Van

BR dual-heated stock
Up working: Perth dep 21.00

One of the TPOs which has operated for many years is that between Carlisle and Perth. This is worked by a single PO Sorting Van and is known to the Post Office as the Caledonian TPO Down Day. Departure time has always been about 20.30. In prewar days, the PO Van was attached to the 17.00 from Manchester/Liverpool to Scotland. In 1927 the train also carried two coaches from Euston (dep 13.30) to Aberdeen. At this time the train was divided at Beattock into portions for Glasgow/Edinburgh and Aberdeen which departed at 21.28 and 21.38 respectively. Two Milk Vans and two Brake Vans for Dundee were added behind the PO Van during the stop. In 1938 the two Dundee Brake Vans were attached at Lockerbie and the train divided at Carstairs. Incidentally, the Restaurant Car from Manchester was still diagrammed for a pre-grouping vehicle in 1938. After the war the PO Van was attached to the front of the portion for Edinburgh. During the winter timetable the 20.22 from Carlisle was down to a three-coach formation: PO Sorting Van/Corr Composite/Corr Brake Third. The working was changed in the early 1950s with the train becoming an independent departure. However, the opportunity was taken to attach the PO Van to the 13.35 Euston-Perth when this was introduced at the beginning of the 1954 winter timetable. This arrangement continued until 1966 when the train again became an independent working. It has remained this way ever since.

Left:
Rebuilt 'Patriot' 4-6-0 No 45527 *Southport* leaves Gleneagles on a 1.26pm Carlisle-Perth service in July 1964. *W. J. V. Anderson*

09.45 Glasgow-Oban

1927

Glasgow dep 09.45

BC	BC	C	B3	C3	OB

Brake Composite
Brake Composite } (ex-Edinburgh)*
Composite
Brake Third
Corr Third
Observation Car

Up working: Oban dep 15.45

1938

Glasgow dep 09.45

BC	C3	B3	O3	O3	RC	O1	B3

Brake Composite 60ft
Corr Third (64) } (ex-Edinburgh)*
Open Brake Third
Open Third (42)
Open Third (42)
Restaurant Composite
Open First (42)
Open Brake Third

Up working: Oban dep 15.40

1949

Glasgow dep 08.00

BC	CC	O3	B3	CC	B3

Corr Brake Composite (12/21) — (ex-Edinburgh)*
Corr Composite (18/24)
Open Third (56)
Inter-Corr Set

LMS stock
Up working: Oban dep 17.15

1958

Glasgow dep 07.55

BC	C2	CC	B2	CC	B2	O2	OB

Corr Brake Composite (12/21) — (ex-Edinburgh)*
Corr Second (42) (ThFO)
Corr Composite (18/24)
Corr Brake Second (24)
Corr Composite (18/24)
Corr Brake Second (24)
Open Second (56)
Observation Car

LMS stock
Up working: Oban dep 17.25

1964

Glasgow dep 07.55

BC	C2	C2	C2	CC	B2	O2	OB

Corr Brake Composite
Corr Second } (ex-Edinburgh)*
Corr Second
Corr Second
Corr Composite
Corr Brake Second
Open Second
Observation Car

BR Mk 1 stock
Up working: Oban dep 17.30

1973
Glasgow dep 08.35

C2	CC	B2	BU	CC	O2

Corr Second
Corr Composite
Corr Brake Second
Miniature Buffet
Corr Composite
Tourist Open Second

BR Mk 1 stock
Up working: Oban dep 17.40

1984
Glasgow dep 08.20

C2	C2	B2	C2	B2	SA

Corr Second
Corr Second
Open Brake Second Micro-Buffet
Corr Second
Corr Brake Second
Saloon

BR Mk 1 stock
Up working: Oban dep 13.00

* attached at Callander

One of the new Pullman cars delivered to the Caledonian Railway in 1914 was the Observation Car *Maid of Morven*. It was assigned to the 09.45 Glasgow-Oban service and spent all its life on this duty. Presumably the other coaches in the 1927 formation shown were built by the Caledonian. Four of them were non-corridor vehicles, including the two which had come from Edinburgh. The Observation Car was withdrawn from service in December 1937. The following year the train was formed from modern open stock leaving Glasgow; the two coaches from Edinburgh were of the side corridor type. One of the early results of the formation of British Railways was a morning train from Glasgow (Queen Street) to Oban. Consequently the starting time of the 09.45 was put back by about two hours, and the refreshment car was absent from the train. In 1958 one of the Pullman Observation Cars from the defunct 'Devon Belle' was repainted maroon and was put to work in the 07.55 to Oban. LMS stock regularly formed the set into the 1960s but by 1964 it had been replaced by BR standard coaches. The Observation Car was withdrawn in 1967 and a Miniature Buffet was subsequently added to the set. Mk 1 stock has continued to work on the line during the past 20 years.

Left:
One daily train which was still diagrammed for all-LMS stock in 1960 was the 12.05 Oban-Glasgow/Edinburgh. It is shown arriving at Killin Junction in May 1960 made up of Period 3 coaches behind 'Black Five' No 45125. The third, fourth and fifth vehicles (B3, CC, B3) constituted an inter-corridor set. Behind was one of the LMS Restaurant Composites which had been allocated to Scotland in the 1930s. *M. Mensing*

10.00 Glasgow-Aberdeen (The 'Granite City')

1927

Glasgow dep 10.00

C	**C3**	**BC**	**B3**	**C3**	**PK**	**CC**	**B3**

Composite (FO) } Perth
Corr Third } Perth
Corr Brake Composite — Inverness
Corr Brake Third } Aberdeen
Corr Third } Aberdeen
Pullman } Aberdeen
Corr Composite } Aberdeen
Corr Brake Third } Aberdeen

Up working: Aberdeen dep 17.30

1938

Glasgow dep 10.05

B3	**C3**	**CC**	**R3**	**OC**	**CC**	**C3**	**B3**	**B3**	**CC**	**B3**

Corr Brake Third (40) } *
Corr Third (64) } *
Corr Composite (18/32) } *
Restaurant Third (30)
Open Composite (18/18)

Corr Composite (18/32) } *
Corr Third (64) } *
Corr Brake Third (40) } *
Inter-Corr Set

* Clipped sets of three vehicles each
Up working: Aberdeen dep 15.20

1949

Glasgow dep 10.00

C3	**C3**	**B3**	**C3**	**CC**	**CC**	**RC**	**O3**	**CC**	**B3**	**BV**

Corr Third (42)
Corr Third (42)
Corr Brake Third (24)
Corr Third (42)
Corr Composite (18/24)
Corr Composite (18/24)
Restaurant Composite (12/18)

Open Third (56)
Corr Composite (18/24)
Corr Brake Third (24)
Brake Van

LMS stock
Up working: Aberdeen dep 17.30

1958

Glasgow dep 10.15

B2	**C2**	**C1**	**RC**	**O2**	**C2**	**C2**	**B2**	**BV**

Corr Brake Second
Corr Second
Corr First
Restaurant Composite (12/18) (LMS)
Open Second
Corr Second

Corr Second
Corr Brake Second
Brake Van

BR Mk 1 stock
Up working: Aberdeen dep 17.25

1964

Glasgow dep 10.00

C2	**B2**	**C2**	**C2**	**C2**	**RU**	**C1**	**B1**

Corr Second (ThFO)
Corr Brake Second
Corr Second
Corr Second
Corr Second
Restaurant Unclassified (33)

Corr First
Corr Brake Second

BR Mk 1 stock
Up working: Aberdeen dep 17.15

1973
Glasgow dep 08.10

B2	O2	O2	BU	C1	B2

Open Brake Second
Tourist Open Second
Tourist Open Second
Miniature Buffet
Corr First
Corr Brake Second

BR Mk 1 stock
Up working: Aberdeen dep 13.15

1984
Glasgow dep 09.25

O2	O2	O2	O2	O1	B2

Tourist Open Second
Tourist Open Second
Tourist Open Second
Tourist Open Second Micro-Buffet
Open First
Open Brake Second (BR Mk 2A)

BR Mk 2 air-conditioned stock
Up working: Aberdeen dep 13.25

The Caledonian Railway had built their six-wheel bogied 'Grampian' corridor stock for the morning service to Aberdeen. Some of these vehicles may well have been included in the formation shown for June 1927. Unfortunately the contemporary Carriage Marshalling book does not indicate seating requirements. A Pullman car had gone into the train in 1914 to provide a Restaurant Car service. One of the original cars supplied to the Caledonian, *Lass o'Gowrie*, was assigned to the train in 1927. A Brake Composite for Inverness was carried to Perth; during July and August, Inverness was given a separate train from Glasgow.

During the next 10 years the train was converted over to LMS-built stock so that in 1938 it was made up of Period 1 and 2 style coaches. Two three-coach sets in the train were 'clipped' together to enable the sets to be kept intact. A device was fixed to the drawbar hook over the coupling link, in such a manner that the coaches could not easily be separated. Several new Third Class Restaurant Cars had gone to the Northern Division in the mid-1930s and one replaced the Pullman car on the 10.05.

After the war an LMS Restaurant Composite was used, the remainder of the set being mostly Period 3 design coaches. For example, in April 1955 the following were in the set: Corridor Brake Third M5943M, Open Third M8854M, Restaurant Composite SC251M, Corridor Composite SC24622M, Corridor Brake Third SC26514M, Corridor Composite SC4428M, Corridor Brake Third M5706M.

Apart from a Period 2 Open Third, all the vehicles were Period 3 designs; the large proportion of vehicles allocated to the LM Region is notable. Within three years the only LMS coach remaining was the Restaurant Composite, the remainder of the set having changed to BR standard stock. A BR standard Restaurant Unclassified soon replaced the LMS vehicle. From February 1966 a BR Griddle Car, converted from a Restaurant First, was used for meal service. The train was withdrawn in September 1967, and the 08.10 remained as the only morning departure to Aberdeen. Mk 1 stock continued to be used for several years as Mk 2 coaches did not begin to go into the service until 1975.

As shown by the 1984 formation, Mk 2 air-conditioned stock eventually arrived. Two other Aberdeen sets had the same formation at this time. The following year, the Glasgow-Aberdeen day trains were worked with Mk 3 push-pull sets.

Above:
The 10.00 Glasgow-Aberdeen approaching Aberdeen in October 1951. The leading coach was a Period 1 Corridor Third but the remainder visible were Period 3 including two post-nationalisation coaches with porthole windows. Pickersgill Caledonian 4-4-0 No 54450 pilots BR Standard Class 5 4-6-0 No 73005. *W. J. V. Anderson*

Below:
Standard Class 5MT 4-6-0 No 73007 leaves Perth for Aberdeen with the 'Granite City' on 22 July 1952. *R. K. Evans*

Above:
The same train is shown a decade later, in May 1964, returning to Glasgow as the 17.30 from Aberdeen. The seven-coach set is BR standard stock including the unclassified Restaurant Car. Class A4 Pacific No 60009 *Union of South Africa* is in charge. *W. J. V. Anderson*

Below:
On 24 May 1976 the 10.10 Glasgow-Aberdeen service passes Dunblane behind Class 25 No 25087. The train is made up from BR Mk 1 and 2 stock. *Brian Morrison*

12.30 Glasgow-Stranraer

1927

Glasgow dep 12.30

C3	C3	N1	C3	BV	CC	B3	B3	PK	BC	O3

Corr Third — Girvan

Corr Third
First
Corr Third
Brake Van
} Stranraer

Corr Composite
Corr Brake Third
Brake Third
Pullman
Corr Brake Composite
Third (TO)
} Ayr

Down working: Stranraer dep 12.25

1938

Glasgow dep 12.30

B3	CC	B3	RU	B3	C	B3

Inter-Corr 3-Set — Stranraer

Restaurant Car
Inter-Corr 3-Set
} Ayr

Down working: Stranraer dep 12.30

1949

Glasgow dep 12.25

C3	CC	B3	CC	B3	C	3	3

Corr Third (42)
Corr Composite (18/24)
Inter-Corr Set
} Stranraer

Composite (24/72)
Third (54)
Third (54)
} Ayr

LMS stock

Down working: Stranraer dep 09.15

1958

Glasgow dep 12.30

B2	CC	C2	CC	B2	B2	C	B2

Corr Brake Second (24)
Corr Composite (18/24)
Corr Second (24)
Corr Composite (18/24)
Corr Brake Second (24)
} Stranraer

Brake Second (84)
Composite (32/36)
Brake Second (84)
} Ayr

LMS stock

Down working: Stranraer dep 11.44

1960

Glasgow dep 12.30

Mb	TB	M2	M2	TC	Mb	M2	TC	Mb

Motor Brake Second
Buffet Trailer First
Motor Second
} Stranraer

Motor Second
Trailer Composite
Motor Brake Second
} Girvan

Motor Second (WO)
Trailer Composite (WO)
Motor Brake Second (WO)
} Ayr

Diesel Multiple Unit

Down working: Stranraer dep 16.25

1964
Glasgow dep 11.25

Mb	**TC**	**M2**	**M2**	**TC**	**Mb**

Motor Brake Second
Trailer Composite
Motor Second
Motor Second
Trailer Composite
Motor Brake Second

Diesel Multiple Unit
Down working: Stranraer dep 16.25

1984
Glasgow dep 11.30

C2	**C2**	**C2**	**B2**	**C2**	**C2**

Corr Second
Corr Second
Corr Second
Open Brake Second
Corr Second
Corr Second

BR Mk 1 stock
Down working: Stranraer dep 18.35

The G&SWR did not provide dining facilities on their Stranraer trains. They were introduced by the LMS in 1923 when a Pullman was attached as far as Ayr on the 12.30 from St Enoch. It returned to Glasgow on the late morning train from Stranraer, thus supplying lunch to both trains. The Pullman car allocated in 1927 was *Lass o'Ballochmyle*. It was one of three Pullmans built by the Clayton Wagon Company in 1923 for LMS Scottish services. It was 63ft 10in in length and could seat 33 passengers. The remainder of the coaches in the 1927 formation would most likely have been of pre-grouping origin; a Non-Corridor First was included in the Stranraer portion. In 1938 the train consisted of two Inter-Corridor 3-sets each made up of Brake Third/Composite/Brake Third. They were probably made up from pre-grouping stock but early LMS coaches may have been included. One Inter-Corridor Set was detached at Ayr along with the Restaurant Car which had remained a Pullman but was now owned by the LMS and painted in that company's livery.

Restaurant Cars did not reappear after the war. LMS stock was still used in 1958, all the Glasgow-Stranraer portions having the same formation as shown for the 12.30. Cross-country Diesel Multiple Units built at Swindon took over the service in 1959/60. A First Class Trailer fitted with buffet area was in the sets when they first appeared but it seems unlikely that they were ever used for refreshments and these coaches were soon transferred away. DMUs worked the service until May 1982 when locomotive-hauled sets of Mk 1 vehicles returned to the line. A new Sealink livery was applied to the coaches during the following two years to emphasise their connecting role with the shipping service from Stranraer.

Right:
A Glasgow-Stranraer train, again at Ayr, in the 1950s. The leading Stranraer portion was made up of Period 1 and Period 3 coaches. The rear non-corridor set would have been detached at Ayr. 'Jubilee' 4-6-0 No 45687 *Neptune* is in charge.
Real Photographs K3792

10.10 Inverness-Wick/Thurso

1927

Inverness dep 10.10

BV	PS	R1	CC	CC	C3	BV	BC

Brake Van — Wick†
PO Sorting Van — Helmsdale*
Restaurant First } Helmsdale
Corr Composite } Helmsdale
Corr Composite } Wick
Corr Third } Wick
Brake Van } Wick

Corr Brake Composite — Thurso

Up working: Wick dep 15.05

1938

Inverness dep 10.25

BV	PS	RC	CC	CC	C3	BV	BC	C3	BC

Brake Van — Wick†
PO Sorting Van — Helmsdale*
Common Restaurant } Helmsdale
Corr Composite (18/32) } Helmsdale
Corr Composite (18/32) } Wick
Corr Third (64) } Wick
Brake Van } Wick

Corr Brake Composite (12/32) } Thurso
Corr Third (64) } Thurso
Brake Composite — Strathpeffer

Up working: Wick dep 15.30

1949

Inverness dep 10.40

PS	RC	B3	CC	B3	CC	BV	CC	B3

PO Sorting Van — Helmsdale*
Restaurant Composite (12/18) — Helmsdale
Inter-Corr Set } Wick
Corr Composite (18/24) } Wick
Brake Van } Wick

Corr Composite (18/24) } Thurso
Corr Brake Third (24) } Thurso

LMS stock
Up working: Wick dep 08.25

1958

Inverness dep 10.40

PS	RB	B2	CC	B2	CC	BV	CC	B2

PO Sorting Van — Helmsdale*
Buffet (24) — Helmsdale
Corr Brake Second (24) } Wick
Corr Composite (18/24) } Wick
Corr Brake Second (24) } Wick
Corr Composite (18/24) } Wick
Brake Van } Wick

Corr Composite (18/24) } Thurso
Corr Brake Second (24) } Thurso

LMS stock
Up working: Wick dep 08.35

1964

Inverness dep 10.30

PS	B2	CC	BU	C2	BV	CC	C2

PO Sorting Van — Helmsdale†
Corr Brake Second (BR1) } Wick
Corr Composite (BR1) } Wick
Miniature Buffet (BR1) } Wick
Corr Second (BR1) } Wick

Brake Van (LMS) } Thurso
Corr Composite (18/24) (LMS) } Thurso
Corr Second (42) (LMS) } Thurso

Up working: Wick dep 17.00

1973

Inverness dep 10.50

BC	BV	CS	CC	C2

Corr Brake Composite — Wick
Brake Van
Corr Second
Corr Composite
Corr Second
} Thurso

BR Mk 1 stock
Up working: Wick dep 17.33

1984

Inverness dep 11.35

B2	O2	O2	BV	O2

Open Brake Second Micro-Buffet
Tourist Open Second
} Wick

Tourist Open Second
Brake Van
Tourist Open Second
} Thurso

BR Mk 1 stock
Up working: Wick dep 18.00

* from Perth — attached Dingwall
† from Perth

Gangwayed corridor stock was rostered for the 10.10 northbound train from Inverness in 1927; the same was true for the 06.15 from Inverness. The Highland Railway, however, had built less than 30 coaches with gangways. To remedy this shortage of gangwayed stock, the LMS transferred appropriate coaches to the Highland lines soon after amalgamation. They included vehicles built by the LNWR, CR, L&Y, MR and FR. Some of these would have been represented in the 10.10 in 1927; the assigned Restaurant Car came from the Midland Railway. The Post Office Sorting Van which started at Perth was a Highland vehicle. The formation was essentially the same 10 years later but by this time LMS Period 1 and 2 stock was rostered. The 'Common' designation for the restaurant car indicated it was for use by First and Second Class passengers. An L&Y 65ft 6in Restaurant First was regularly employed on this working in the 1930s. A Non-Corridor Brake Composite for Strathpeffer, probably built by the Highland Railway, was removed at Dingwall. The Highland Mail Van working had been changed by this time, for Post Office purposes. Leaving Inverness on the preceding Kyle train, it was detached at Dingwall and picked up by the Wick train.

A Restaurant Car was provided after the war, an old Midland clerestory-roofed vehicle (LMS No 180) being used around 1950. It was soon withdrawn and a LMS Pullman took over for several years; a LNER Buffet Car was then used for a while. Period 3 LMS passenger stock was mainly used after the war and was still employed in the early 1960s. By 1964 the Wick portion, now with a Miniature Buffet, and been reformed with BR standard stock, but that for Thurso was still LMS. A Highland Mail Van, built in 1916, was assigned until 1961 when new BR standard vans (Nos SC80315-7) appeared. This must have been one of the few instances where a pre-grouping vehicle regularly worked behind a BR diesel locomotive. This mail working to Helmsdale ceased in 1967. Standard Mk 1 stock has been used on the line for the last 20 years.

Right:
Crossing at Kildary in August 1959 are the 10.40 Inverness-Wick/Thurso and the 12.05 Tain-Inverness. The Inverness-bound train was made up of a Period 1 and Period 3 coaches and headed by ex-Caledonian 4-4-0 No 54470.
W. A. C. Smith

10.20 Inverness-Kyle of Lochalsh

1927
Inverness dep 10.20

C	B3	CC	B3	BV

Composite — (ex-Dingwall)
Corr Brake Third
Corr Composite
Corr Brake Third
Brake Van (non-gangway)

Up working: Kyle dep 11.00

1938
Inverness dep 10.15

PS	BV	CC	CC	RC	O3	O3	BV

PO Sorting Van — Dingwall
Brake Van
Corr Composite (18/32)
Corr Composite (18/32)
Common Restaurant
Open Third (42)
Open Third (42)
Brake Van

Up working: Kyle dep 17.35

1949
Inverness dep 10.30

PS	BV	BV	C3	CC	CC	C3	BV

PO Sorting Van — Dingwall
Brake Van
Brake Van
Corr Third (42)
Corr Composite (18/24)
Corr Composite (18/24)
Corr Third (42)
Brake Van

LMS stock
Up working: Kyle dep 10.45

1958
Inverness dep 10.30

BV	PS	B2	CC	CC	C2	C2	BV	C2	RC

Brake Van
PO Sorting Van — Dingwall
Corr Brake Second (24)
Corr Composite (18/24)
Corr Composite (18/24)
Corr Second (42)
Corr Second (42)
Brake Van
Corr Second (42)
Restaurant Composite (12/18) — Achnasheen

LMS stock
Up working: Kyle dep 10.45

1964
Inverness dep 10.30

B2	CC	CC	C2	BV

Corr Brake Second
Corr Composite
Corr Composite
Corr Second
Brake Van

BR Mk 1 stock
Up working: Kyle dep 17.30

1973
Inverness dep 10.36

B2	CC	C2	BV	O2

Corr Brake Second
Corr Composite
Corr Second
Brake Van
Tourist Open Second

BR Mk 1 stock
Up working: Kyle dep 17.50

1984
Inverness dep 10.45

O2	BV	O2	O2	B2	O2

Tourist Open Second
Brake Van
Tourist Open Second
Tourist Open Second
Open Brake Second Micro-Buffet
Tourist Open Second

BR Mk 1 stock
Up working: Kyle dep 17.10

Although gangwayed corridor stock was rostered for the Kyle train in 1927, refreshments could not be obtained until the following year when a Tea Car began to run to Achnasheen. This duty was performed by an old Midland Open Third Restaurant car No 3898 (3899 was the standby). It was replaced in 1929 by an L&Y Restaurant First, Nos 10799 and 10800 (later renumbered 80/1) which had recently arrived on the Highland from Lancashire. The other stock at this time could have come from several sources as noted for the 10.10 Inverness-Wick/Thurso train (a PO Sorting Van working north of Inverness is also discussed for the 10.10 train). The Composite attached at Dingwall returned the following morning as the only passenger vehicle on the 06.10 mixed train from Kyle. Restaurant Car working was changed in 1935 with the vehicle going through to Kyle during the summer instead of being transferred to the up train at Achnasheen. The seating requirements for the 1938 formation indicate the use of LMS-built stock but pre-grouping vehicles could still have appeared. At Kyle the train was remarshalled with the stock off the 07.25 from Inverness to form the 17.35 and the following days' 10.45 departures. The Restaurant Car at this time would probably have been a L&Y vehicle but an LMS-owned Pullman was possible.

When dining facilities returned to the line in 1950 the service was provided by the last remaining L&Y car (LMS No 82) in LMS livery. Following its withdrawal in May 1951 a Restaurant Composite, often a former Pullman vehicle, was substituted. LMS corridor coaches, mainly of Period 3 design, were used throughout the 1950s and early 1960s but the 1964 set consisted solely of BR standard stock. One of the Observation Cars from the 'Devon Belle' was employed on the train during the 1960s (when the summer relief to Kyle did not run) until withdrawn in 1967. Refreshment facilities were absent from the train (and line) for 10 years, until a Miniature Buffet was added for the summer of 1977. It was still provided in 1983, along with Mk 1 coaches, but replaced by a Micro-Buffet the following year.

Right:
The 10.45 Kyle of Lochalsh-Inverness, the 'Hebridean', at Dingwall in 1939 headed by ex-Highland Railway Cumming 4-6-0 No 17954. A standard LMS Brake Van led the train followed by an L&Y Restaurant Car. The remainder of the train was Period 1 stock. *M. W. Earley*

10.20 Leeds-Glasgow

1927

Leeds dep 10.20

BV	C3	RC	BC	BC	BV	C3	CC	B3	MV

Brake Van — (ex-Lugton)
Corr Third } (ex-Carlisle)
Restaurant Composite } (ex-Carlisle)
Corr Brake Composite — (ex-Manchester)
Corr Composite Brake — (ex-Sheffield)
Brake Van

Corr Third (MO)
Corr Composite
Corr Brake Third
Milk Van — (ex-Kirkcudbright)

Up working: Glasgow dep 17.30

1938

Leeds dep 10.20

BV	BC	C3	O3	R1	BC	B3	CC

Brake Van
Corr Brake Composite (9/21) — (ex-Manchester)
Corr Third (42)
Open Third (42)
Restaurant First (24)

Corr Brake Composite (12/32)
Corr Brake Third (24) (LNER) } Edinburgh
Corr Composite (18/32) (LNER) } Edinburgh

Up working: Glasgow dep 17.30

1949

Leeds dep 10.25

O3	O3	B3	CC	CC	CC	C3	B3	O3	RC	OC

Open Third (56) (MFO)
Open Third (56)
Corr Brake Third (24)
Corr Composite (18/24)
Corr Composite (18/24)
Corr Composite (18/24)
Corr Third (42)

Corr Brake Third (24)
Open Third (56)
Restaurant Composite (12/18) } Dumfries
Open Composite (18/18) } Dumfries

LMS stock
Up working: Glasgow dep 16.00

1955

Leeds dep 10.35

BV	C3	B3	C3	CC	CC	C3	C3	B3	R1	OC

Brake Van (MX)
Corr Third (42) (LMS) (MFO)
Corr Brake Third (24) (LMS)
Corr Third (42) (LMS)
Corr Composite (BR1)
Corr Composite (BR1)
Corr Third (42) (LMS)

Corr Third (42) (LMS)
Corr Brake Third (24) (LMS)
Restaurant First (24) } Kilmarnock
Open Composite (18/18) (LMS) } Kilmarnock

Up working: Glasgow dep 16.00

1963

Leeds dep 10.35

BV	B2	C2	C2	RB	O2	CC	CC	C2	C2	B2

Brake Van
Corr Brake Second
Corr Second
Corr Second
Restaurant Buffet (23)
Open Second
Corr Composite

Corr Composite
Corr Second
Corr Second
Corr Brake Second

BR Mk 1 stock
Up working: Glasgow dep 16.00

1973

Leeds dep 09.46

BV	BC	CC	RU	O2	O2	C2	C2

Brake Van
Corr Brake Composite
Corr Composite
Restaurant Unclassified (33)
Tourist Open Second
Tourist Open Second
Corr Second
Corr Second

BR Mk 1 stock supplied by ER
Up working: Glasgow dep 15.25

1981

Nottingham dep 07.15

BV	C2	O2	CC	RB	O2	C2	B2

Brake Van
Corr Second
Tourist Open Second
Corr Composite
Restaurant Buffet (18)
Tourist Open Second
Corr Second
Corr Brake Second

BR dual-heated 100mph stock
Up working: Glasgow dep 15.50

The origins of this train date back into Midland Railway history; through carriages for Glasgow and Edinburgh were being carried on the 10.00 from Leeds in 1903. The formation north of Carlisle is shown for 1927. A Brake Composite from Manchester (Victoria) to Glasgow had been added at Hellifield, this being a continuation of the working instituted in conjunction with the L&Y. Three coaches for Edinburgh (Waverley), a Composite and a Brake Third from Leeds and a Locker Composite from Manchester (Victoria) were dropped at Carlisle. A Restaurant Car was attached at Carlisle — the rostered car in 1927 being No 18588 (later No 299), a clerestory roof Composite built by the G&SWR in 1921. The set returned from St Enoch at 17.30 along with the Restaurant Car. There were two Brakes Composite on the rear, one for Bradford and the other for Bristol. A Post Office Tender Van, from Ayr, was attached to the front at Kilmarnock. In the following year the Restaurant Car circuit was changed so that the car worked through from Leeds to Glasgow. Initially a WCJS composite built in 1897 to Diagram 10 was used. The 1938 set consisted of modern LMS stock including one of the 68ft First Class Restaurant Cars partnered by an Open Third. The use of LNER stock to Edinburgh is notable. These coaches returned to Leeds in a separate train.

The set had grown in size by 1949 even though the through coaches to Edinburgh, and from Manchester, were no longer carried. The Restaurant Car working had also changed, a Composite type and partner Open Composite being removed at Dumfries (Kilmarnock from 1951). BR standard stock had started to go into the set in 1955 and the Restaurant Car was replaced by a First Class vehicle in the same year. By 1958 all the vehicles, except the two used for dining, were rostered to have been replaced by BR standards of the same class as shown for 1955. This formation remained the same for a few years although the Restaurant Car reverted to a Composite in the 1960 winter timetable, and started to work through to Glasgow in 1962. The 1963 formation showed a slight rearrangement of the stock but otherwise was the same as 10 years earlier, allowing of course for the use of BR standard coaches. The same is basically true of the 1975 set but by now the size had been reduced. From 1976 the train departed from Nottingham instead of Leeds. Starting in 1982 the train was rerouted via Manchester and the West Coast main line and all contact with Leeds was severed.

09.47 Liverpool (Exchange)-Glasgow/Edinburgh

1923

Liverpool dep 09.47

BC	BV	B3	CC	C3	B3	C3	CC	RC	CC	B3	B3	CC	BC

Corr Brake Composite 57ft (WCJS) — Southport-Glasgow

Brake Van 50ft (WCJS) Corr Brake Third 57ft (WCJS) Corr Composite 57ft (WCJS) Corr Third (MFO) 57ft (WCJS)	Manchester-Glasgow
Corr Brake Third Corr Third 50ft Corr Composite 57ft (WCJS) Restaurant Composite 65ft (WCJS) Corr Composite 57ft (WCJS) Corr Brake Third 57ft (WCJS)	Liverpool-Glasgow
Corr Brake Third 57ft (WCJS) Corr Composite 57ft (WCJS)	Liverpool-Edinburgh
Corr Brake Composite 57ft (WCJS) (MFO)	Manchester-Edinburgh

Up working: Glasgow dep 10.10

1934

Liverpool dep 09.45

BC	C3	CC	B3	C3	O3	R1	CC	B3	CC	B3

Corr Brake Composite (12/32) — Manchester-Edinburgh

Corr Third (64) Corr Composite (18/32) Corr Brake Third (24)	Manchester-Glasgow
Corr Third (64) (MO) Open Third 60ft Restaurant First 65ft Corr Composite (18/32) Corr Brake Third (24)	Liverpool-Glasgow
Corr Composite (18/24) Corr Brake Third (24)	Liverpool-Edinburgh

Up working: Glasgow dep 09.25

1949

Liverpool dep 09.40

O3	B3	R3	OC	CC	CC	B3	B3	CC	CC	B3

Open Third (56) Corr Brake Third (24) Restaurant Third (30) Open Composite (18/18) Corr Composite (18/24) Corr Composite (18/24) Corr Brake Third (24)	Glasgow
Corr Brake Third (24) Corr Composite (18/24) Corr Composite (18/24) Corr Brake Third (24)	Edinburgh

LMS stock

Up working: Glasgow dep 10.35

1958

Liverpool dep 08.57

B2	O2	RC	C1	C2	C2	B2	C2	B2	CC	B2

Corr Brake Second (24) (LMS) Open Second (56) (LMS) Restaurant Composite (12/18) (LMS) Corr First (36) Corr Second (BR1) Corr Second (BR1) Corr Brake Second (BR1)	Glasgow
Corr Second (42) (LMS) Corr Brake Second (BR1) Corr Composite (BR1) Corr Brake Second (BR1)	Edinburgh

Up working: Glasgow dep 10.55

1963

Liverpool dep 09.50

B2	CC	O2	B2	O2	R1	CC	B2	O2	B2	CC

Corr Brake Second (24) (LMS)
Corr Composite (18/24) (LMS)
Open Second (56) (LMS)
Corr Brake Second (24) (LMS)
Open Second (BR1)
Restaurant First (24) (LMS)
Corr Composite (BR1)
Corr Brake Second (24) (LMS)
} Glasgow

Open Second (56) (LMS)
Corr Brake Second (24) (LMS)
Corr Composite (18/24) (LMS)
} Edinburgh

Up working: Glasgow dep 11.30

1975

Liverpool dep 09.41

B1	O2	O2	O2	C1	C1	BV

Corr Brake First
Tourist Open Second
Tourist Open Second
Tourist Open Second
Corr First
Corr First
Brake Van

BR Mk 2 air-braked stock
Up working: Glasgow dep 16.40

1983

Liverpool dep 09.30

B2	CC	O2	O2	B2	CC	O2	O2

Corr Brake Second
Corr Composite
Tourist Open Second
Tourist Open Second
Corr Brake Second
} Glasgow

Corr Composite
Tourist Open Second
Tourist Open Second
} Edinburgh

BR dual-heated 100mph stock
Up working: Glasgow dep 16.20

The practice of joining/dividing the Liverpool/Manchester morning trains for Glasgow/Edinburgh at Preston and Carstairs which had been established by the LNWR was continued by the LMS. The 1923 train was formed, as might be expected, of WCJS vehicles. The through Brake Composite from Southport to Glasgow is noteworthy but apparently was discontinued soon afterwards. The formation in the mid-1930s was somewhat similar but now consisted mainly of Period 1 (or pre-grouping) stock with later styles just beginning to appear. By 1938 the formation had a large proportion of Period 3 vehicles. An interesting feature of the prewar working was that a Brake Composite from Whithorn to Edinburgh, which travelled via Dumfries, was attached to the rear at Lockerbie. On certain days it was accompanied by a similar coach which came from Stranraer.

After the war the Liverpool and Manchester trains ran separately to Scotland although in later years they were combined during the winter timetable. BR standard stock was quite late in appearing, the 1954 set being essentially the same as shown for 1949. Even in 1963 most of the train consisted of LMS coaches and it was not until about 1965 that BR stock was exclusively used. During the last decade the train has undergone many changes, the formation and destination (Glasgow and/or Edinburgh) changing almost from year to year.

Above:
In the summer of 1954 the two portions of the 14.00 Manchester/Liverpool-Glasgow combined train ran separately on a Saturday. The Saturdays-only version from Manchester is shown, at Tebay, which probably explains the presence of pre-1933 coaches in the front Glasgow portion; the rear five went to Edinburgh. 'Jubilee' 4-6-0 No 45677 *Beatty* heads the train. *J. E. Wilkinson*

Below:
About half of the morning train from Manchester to Glasgow was regularly made up with LMS coaches in 1960/61. The train is shown at Crawford headed by rebuilt 'Royal Scot' 4-6-0 No 46104 *Scottish Borderer* in July 1961. *Derek Cross*

10.55 Liverpool (Exchange)-Newcastle

1929

Liverpool dep 10.55

BV	C3	C1	O3	R1	C3	B3

Brake Van
Corr Third
Corr First
Open Third
Restaurant First
Corr Third
Corr Brake Third

Up working: Newcastle dep 16.50

1935

Liverpool dep 10.45

BV	C3	O3	O3	R1	B1

Brake Van
Corr Third
Open Third
Open Third
Restaurant First
Corr Brake First

Up working: Newcastle dep 17.00

1949

Liverpool dep 10.45

BV	O3	CC	CC	R1	O3	O3	O3	B3

Brake Van
Open Third (56)
Corr Composite (18/24)
Corr Composite (18/24)
Restaurant First (24)
Open Third (56)
Open Third (56)
Open Third (56)
Corr Brake Third (24)

LMS stock
Up working: Newcastle dep 17.00

1954

Liverpool dep 10.30

BV	C3	CC	CC	R1	O3	C3	C3	B3

Brake Van
Corr Third (42)
Corr Composite (18/24)
Corr Composite (18/24)
Restaurant First (24)
Open Third (56)
Corr Third (42)
Corr Third (42)
Corr Brake Third (24)

LMS stock
Up working: Newcastle dep 17.10

1960

Liverpool dep 10.30

BV	C2	CC	CC	BU	O2	O2	O2	B2	O2

Brake Van (LMS)
Corr Second (42) (LMS)
Corr Composite (BR1)
Corr Composite (BR1)
Miniature Buffet (BR1)
Open Second (BR1)
Open Second (BR1)
Open Second (BR1)
Brake Second (24) (LMS)
Open Second (56) (LMS) (FO)

Up working: Newcastle dep 17.10

Collaboration between the L&Y and NER resulted in the introduction of a corridor Restaurant Car train between Liverpool and Newcastle in the summer of 1908. As their contribution to the service the L&Y built a six-coach set (the formation was similar to that shown for 1935 except there was a Brake Third instead of a Brake Van). After WW1 the stock appears to have been provided only by the L&Y, and this arrangement was continued by the LMS after grouping. Some LNWR coaches were used in the set around 1925. This included the Restaurant Car, but it soon returned to an L&Y design. By 1935 the train would have been formed from LMS-built stock, the latest style (ie Period 3) being specified for the Restaurant Car. Between 1936 and 1939 a new Restaurant Third and an Open Composite were used for dining.

In 1948 the train was one of 14 selected to be painted in experimental livery during the summer. Chocolate and cream was chosen for the set. The Restaurant Car was not painted in this way because it was absent from the set until the winter timetable. The 1949 formation was maintained through most of the 1950s — the main changes involving the number and type of Thirds. By 1960 the train was mostly made up of BR standard coaches. The following year it terminated at York and there was no refreshment car. In January 1962 four-car Diesel Multiple Units (later Class 110) took over the Manchester-York service and the through working to Liverpool (Exchange) ceased.

Left:
In 1917 the LNWR built two 6-coach sets to work between Liverpool and Newcastle. Almost 40 years later, in August 1955, the 09.00 Liverpool-Newcastle was formed from LMS and BR stock. However, a link with the past was provided by the Kitchen Buffet Car in the centre of the train. It was built as a Restaurant Composite in 1925 with characteristic LNWR styling. Even though converted to a kitchen buffet in 1954 its origin was still apparent. The specified formation at this time was: B3, C3, 2X C1, O3, RB, 2XO3, C3, B3. 'D49' 4-4-9 No 62762 *The Fernie* is piloting 'V2' 2-6-2 No 60893. *J. C. W. Halliday*

Left:
Nearly 20 years later, in March 1971, the corresponding up train is shown leaving Newcastle at 15.45 for Liverpool with Mk 1 stock still used in the set. The formation at this time was: BV, CC, C1, RU, 5X02 — one of the Open Seconds being added at a weekend. A Class 40 leads the way. *M. Dunnet*

11.00 Liverpool (Lime Street)-Hull

1934

Liverpool dep 11.00

B3	CC	CC	R1	C3	B3

Corr Brake Third (40)
Corr Composite (18/32)
Corr Composite (18/32)
Restaurant First (20)
Corr Third (56)
Corr Brake Third (40)

Up working: Hull dep 16.00

1949

Liverpool dep 11.00

C3	B3	CC	CC	CC	RB	O3	O3	O3	O3	B3	C3

Corr Third (42)
Corr Brake Third (24)
Corr Composite (18/24)
Corr Composite (18/24)
Corr Composite (18/24)
Buffet (24)
Open Third Twin (56)
Open Third Twin (56)
Corr Brake Third (24)
Corr Third (42)

LMS stock
Up working: Hull dep 16.00

1954

Liverpool dep 11.00

C3	B3	CC	CC	RB	C3	C3	C3	B3

Corr Third
Corr Brake Third
Corr Composite
Corr Composite
Buffet (24) (LMS)
Corr Third
Corr Third
Corr Third
Corr Brake Third

BR Mk 1 stock
Up working: Hull dep 16.02

1960

Liverpool dep 11.00

C2	B2	C1	RC	O2	O2	C2	B2	C2

Corr Second
Corr Brake Second
Corr First
Restaurant Composite (12/18) (LMS)
Second Open
Second Open
Corr Second
Corr Brake Second
Corr Second

BR Mk 1 stock
Up working: Hull dep 16.00

For many years before grouping, LNWR sets worked between Liverpool and Hull. A Restaurant Car service, however, was not provided until 1925. For several years, this was one of the LNWR 65ft clerestory roof vehicles (Nos 10465-71) built around 1900 and later converted to Composites. The partner car was an Open Third. A Restaurant First appeared in 1934, being one of the six LNWR clerestories then remaining from the batch which had been numbered 10398-10412. An 18-seat MR vehicle, probably No 89 or 90, was at work two years later but was soon replaced by an LMS-built Restaurant Composite. With respect to the rest of the formation it would probably have remained as LNWR stock for a few years. LMS-built vehicles were used by 1934, the train being made up from Period 1 and/or Period 2 vehicles. After the war this became the regular load, a 10-coach set being used to Hull. One of the articulated Open Thirds Twin Sets built in 1938 was included. The 1954 set was formed from BR standard stock except for the LMS Buffet Car. The presence of the latter was rather unusual as an LMS Restaurant Composite was usually rostered during the 1950s. 'Trans-Pennine' Diesel Multiple Units took over in 1961.

10.00 Manchester-Bournemouth (The 'Pines Express')

1926
Manchester dep 10.00

B3	CC	R1	O3	C3	CC	B3	BC	C3

Corr Brake Third
Corr Composite
Restaurant First 65ft
Open Third
Corr Third (FO)
} Manchester-Bournemouth

Corr Composite
Corr Brake Third
} Liverpool-Bournemouth**

Corr Brake Composite†
Corr Third (MFO)
} Liverpool-Southampton

MR 54ft stock
Down working: Bournemouth dep 10.20

1938
Manchester dep 10.00

BC	BC	OC	R3	C3	B3	BC	BC

Corr Brake Composite (12/32) — Bradford-Bournemouth*

Corr Brake Composite (12/32)
Open Composite (18/18)
Restaurant Third (30)
Corr Third (42) (FO)
Corr Brake Third (24)
} Manchester-Bournemouth

Corr Brake Composite (12/32) — Liverpool-Bournemouth**
Corr Brake Composite (12/32)† — Liverpool-Southampton**

Down working: Bournemouth dep 10.35

1949
Manchester dep 10.25

B3	CC	BC	CC	CC	RC	O3	O3	O3	C3	B3

Corr Brake Third (24) (MFO)
Corr Composite (18/24) (MFO)
Corr Brake Composite (12/21)
Corr Composite (18/24)
Corr Composite (18/24)
Restaurant Composite (12/18)
Open Third (56)
Open Third (56)
Corr Third (42)
Corr Brake Third (24)

LMS stock
Down working: Bournemouth dep 09.45

1955
Manchester dep 10.25

B3	CC	B3	CC	B3	OC	R3	O3	C3	CC	BC

Corr Brake Third (24)
Corr Composite (18/24)
} (ex-Sheffield)*

Corr Brake Third (24)
Corr Composite (18/24)
} (ex-Liverpool)**

Corr Brake Third (24)
Open Composite (18/18)
Restaurant Third (30)
Open Third (56)
Corr Third (42)
Corr Composite (18/24)
Corr Brake Composite (12/21)

LMS stock
Down working: Bournemouth dep 09.45

1963
Manchester dep 10.00

B2	CC	O2	B2	B2	C2	C2	O2	R1	O2	CC	BC

Corr Brake Second
Corr Composite
Open Second
Corr Brake Second
} (ex-Liverpool)**

Corr Brake Second
Corr Second
Corr Second
Open Second
Restaurant First (24)
Open Second
Corr Composite
Corr Brake Composite

BR Mk 1 stock
Down working: Bournemouth dep 10.00

1983

Manchester dep 09.20

O2	O2	O2	C1	O2	O2	O2	O2	BV

Tourist Open Second
Tourist Open Second
Tourist Open Second
Corr First
Tourist Open Second Micro Buffet
Tourist Open Second
Tourist Open Second
Tourist Open Second
Brake Van

BR Mk 2 air-braked stock
Down working: Poole dep 17.05 to Birmingham
*attached at Birmingham
**attached at Crewe
†LMS and GWR on alternate days

This train was started in 1910 by the LNWR in collaboration with the Midland Railway, travelling via Bath Green Park and the Somerset & Dorset line to Bournemouth. Midland stock was used and, as shown above for 1926, this continued for several years after grouping. There was probably a Brake Composite from Yorkshire in the 1926 set but it would not have been listed in the Carriage Working book referred to. By the early 1930s there was some upgrading of the stock, new LMS cars going into the set. One of the first of the new Restaurant Thirds went into the train in late 1934 replacing a 59ft 18-seat Midland vehicle which had been used for several years. In the same year the Third Class vehicles were replaced with Period 3 designs. The Brake Composite, including the through coach from Bradford, remained as older types until at least 1938. The through coach from Liverpool to Southampton brought a GWR Brake Composite into the train on alternate days. It was detached at Cheltenham, and carried by the GWR over the Midland & South Western Junction line to Southampton. Additional coaches were taken as far as Birmingham but have been omitted for clarity.

The through coach to Southampton did not return when the train was reinstated after the war. In fact, there were no through coaches from Liverpool until 1950. The train continued to consist totally of LMS stock through the mid-1950s but had mostly changed over to BR standard stock by 1958. The LMS Restaurant Third, and partner Open Composite, were retained until replaced by a BR standard Restaurant First in the early 1960s. With the start of the winter 1962 timetable the train was rerouted via Oxford and Reading. By the 1970s the service had been replaced by a Poole-Liverpool working, but from 1979 this train was rerouted to Manchester. The formation shown for 1983 went to Derby after arrival at Poole, returning south the next morning.

Left:
LMS '2P' 4-4-0 No 630 heads the up 'Pines Express' near Masbury Summit in 1936.
L&GRP (135) Courtesy David & Charles

Above:
The same train 24 years later is now loaded to 12 coaches of BR, LNER and LMS origin. Class '2P' 4-4-0 No 40697 pilots BR '9F' 2-10-0 No 92206 past Masbury Halt on 19 August 1960. *Derek Cross*

Below:
With the start of the 1962 winter timetable, the 'Pines Express' was routed away from the Somerset & Dorset route, and instead ran via Basingstoke, Reading and Oxford. In this undated photograph, unrebuilt 'West Country' class Pacific No 34105 *Swanage* traverses Reading West Curve with the northbound service consisting of 11 BR Mk 1 vehicles.
Cecil J. Blay

10.50 Manchester (Exchange)-North Wales

1926

Manchester dep 10.50

BC	BC	BV	C3	CC	UN	UN	UN	UN	UN	UN

Corr Brake Composite 57ft — Portmadoc
Corr Brake Composite 57ft — Pwllheli
Brake Van 50ft — Bangor

Vehicles	Destination
Corr Third 57ft Corr Composite 57ft Manchester and Liverpool Set — 4 vehicles	Llandudno
Holyhead, Manchester and Liverpool Set — 2 vehicles	Holyhead

Up working: Portmadoc dep 12.40

1934

Manchester dep 11.00

B	C	B	B3	CC	R1	O3	C3	UN	UN	CC

3-coach Non-Corr Lavatory Set — Chester

Vehicles	Destination
Corr Brake Third Corr Composite Restaurant First 65ft Open Third 60ft Corr Third Holyhead, Manchester and Liverpool Set — 2 vehicles Corr Composite (WO)	Holyhead

Up working: Holyhead dep 12.27

1949

Manchester dep 10.20

B	C	B	B3	O3	O3	CC	BC	CC	BV

3-coach Non-corr Lavatory Set — Llandudno

Vehicles	Destination
Corr Brake Third (24) Open Third (56) Open Third (56) Corr Composite (18/24) Corr Brake Composite (12/21) Corr Composite (18/24) Brake Van	Holyhead

LMS stock
Up working: Holyhead dep 11.30

1954

Manchester dep 11.55

B3	C3	CC	B3	C3	C3	B3	C3	CC	B3	BV

Vehicles	Destination
Corr Brake Third (24) Corr Third (42) Corr Composite (18/24) Corr Brake Third (24)	Llandudno
Corr Third (42) Corr Third (42) Corr Brake Third (24) Corr Third (42) Corr Composite (18/24) Corr Brake Third (24) Brake Van	Holyhead

LMS stock
Up working: Holyhead dep 19.38 to Birmingham

1963

Manchester dep 11.55

B2	CC	C2	B2	BU	B2	C2	CC	B2

Corr Brake Second (24) (LMS) Corr Composite Corr Second Corr Brake Second	Llandudno
Miniature Buffet Corr Brake Second Corr Second Corr Composite Corr Brake Second (24) (LMS)	Holyhead

BR Mk 1 stock

Up working: Holyhead dep 07.05

1973

Manchester (Victoria) dep 10.20

B2	C2	C2	CC	C2	C2	C2	B2	O2	O2

Corr Brake Second
Corr Second
Corr Second
Corr Composite
Corr Second
Corr Second
Corr Second
Corr Brake Second
Tourist Open Second
Tourist Open Second

BR Mk 1 stock

Up working: Holyhead dep 16.55

1982

Manchester (Victoria) dep 10.45

BV	B2	C2	C2	CC	C2	C2	C2

Brake Van
Corr Brake Second
Corr Second
Corr Second
Corr Composite
Corr Second
Corr Second
Corr Second

BR Mk 1 stock

Up working: Holyhead dep 15.17

The formation for 1926 shown above applied in June: during the peak summer season an LNWR Restaurant Car was also carried to Holyhead. At Chester (dep 12.35), the train was combined with through coaches from Liverpool (dep 10.45). They were a Brake Composite for Portmadoc attached at the front, and five non-corridor coaches for Bangor which were cut in ahead of the centre Brake Van. All the Brake Composites were LNWR types with a brake compartment at each end.

A similar arrangement existed in 1934, three coaches (Corridor Brake Composite, Corridor Composite, Corridor Brake Composite) from Liverpool to Holyhead being attached to the rear at Chester. As the peak season is shown, the Portmadoc and Pwllheli sections, each made up of two coaches, departed from Manchester at 11.15 as a separate train. They were transferred to the front of the 11.40 Liverpool-Afonwen at Chester. The latter train consisted of two Brake Composites for Pwllheli and Portmadoc respectively, separated by a third for Afonwen. A pregrouping Restaurant Car was still in the train as late as 1936 when a 20-seat First was diagrammed.

The train continued after nationalisation but was devoid of through coaches for the Afonwen line and without dining facilities. A portion for Llandudno was carried well into the 1960s. Eventually, a Miniature Buffet was added but did not last for long. The train managed to survive until 1982, albeit made up of Mk 1 stock, being replaced by a Scarborough-Llandudno service in the following year.

11.55 Perth-Inverness

1927
Perth dep 11.55

BC	BC	BC	CC	C3	BV	CC	CC	BV	PK	BC

Corr Brake Composite — Edinburgh-Keith
Corr Brake Composite — Edinburgh-Inverness*
Corr Brake Composite — Glasgow-Inverness*
Corr Composite, Corr Third, Brake Van } Perth-Inverness*
Corr Composite (MO), Corr Composite, Brake Van } Perth-Inverness†
Pullman — Perth-Aviemore
Corr Brake Composite — Perth-Aberfeldy

*via Carr Bridge
†via Forres
Up working: Inverness dep 11.00

1938
Perth dep 11.55 (via Carr Bridge)

BV	B3	CC	B3	CC	B3	R3	OC

Brake Van — Perth-Inverness
Corr Brake Third (40), Corr Composite (18/32) } Edinburgh-Inverness
Inter-Corr Set — Glasgow-Inverness
Restaurant Third (30), Open Composite (18/18) } Glasgow-Aviemore

Perth dep 12.05 (via Forres)

BC	B3	CC	B3	B3	CC	C3	BV	OC	R3

Corr Brake Composite (12/32) — Glasgow-Keith
Inter-Corr Set — Glasgow-Inverness
Corr Brake Third (40), Corr Composite (18/32) } Edinburgh-Inverness
Corr Third (64), Brake Van } Perth-Inverness
Open Composite (18/18), Restaurant Third (30) } Perth-Aviemore

Perth dep 12.10 (via Forres)

BC	BC	C3	C3	CC	BV

Corr Brake Composite (12/32) — Edinburgh-Aviemore
Corr Brake Composite (12/32) — Glasgow-Aviemore
Corr Third (64), Corr Third (64), Corr Composite (18/32), Brake Van } Perth-Inverness

1958
Perth dep 11.51 (Glasgow dep 10.00) (via Carr Bridge)

BV	RC	OC	C2	C2	C2	B2	CC	B2	RC	CC	B2	C2

Brake Van (ThO) — ex-Dundee
Restaurant Composite (12/18) (LMS)*
Open Composite (18/18) (LMS)*
Corr Second
Corr Second (FO)
Corr Second
Corr Brake Second
Corr Composite
Corr Brake Second
Restaurant Composite (12/18) (LMS) — Aviemore
Corr Composite†
Corr Brake Second†
Corr Second†

*attached at Perth
†via Forres: transferred at Aviemore to 10.12 ex-Edinburgh
BR Mk 1 stock
Up working: Inverness dep 15.45

Perth dep 12.05 (Edinburgh dep 10.12) (via Forres)

B2	**CC**	**C2**	**C2**	**RU**	**B2**	**C2**	**CC**	**C2**	**B2**

Corr Brake Second
Corr Composite
Corr Second
Corr Second
Restaurant Unclassified (30) — Aviemore
Corr Brake Second*
Corr Second*
Corr Composite*
Corr Second*
Corr Brake Second*

*via Carr Bridge; transferred at Aviemore to 10.00 ex-Glasgow
BR Mk 1 stock
Up working: Inverness dep 15.20

1964
Perth dep 11.51 (Glasgow dep 09.30)

BV	**RU**	**O2**	**O2**	**RB**	**CC**	**B2**	**C2**	**CC**	**C2**	**C2**	**B2**

Brake Van (ThO) — (ex-Dundee)
Restaurant Unclassified (33) } (ex-Perth)
Restaurant Open Second (48) } (ex-Perth)
Open Second
Restaurant Buffet (23)
Corr Composite
Corr Brake Second
Corr Second
Corr Composite } Edinburgh-Inverness*
Corr Second } Edinburgh-Inverness*
Corr Second } Edinburgh-Inverness*
Corr Brake Second } Edinburgh-Inverness*

*attached at Perth
BR Mk 1 stock
Up working: Inverness dep 16.15

1973
Perth dep 11.04 (Glasgow dep 09.45)

B2	**O2**	**O2**	**RU**	**CC**	**B2**	**O2**	**BC**

Corr Brake Second
Tourist Open Second
Tourist Open Second
Restaurant Unclassified (33)
Corr Composite
Corr Brake Second
Tourist Second Open } Edinburgh-Inverness*
Corr Brake Composite } Edinburgh-Inverness*

*attached at Perth
BR Mk 1 stock
Up working: Inverness dep 16.35

This midday express from Perth had been one of the Highland Railway's most important trains, carrying through coaches from Edinburgh and Glasgow. This necessitated extensive remarshalling at Perth as can be judged from the formation shown for 1927 (June). The Brake Composite from Edinburgh (Waverley) to Inverness would probably have been a LNER-owned vehicle; NBR coaches had worked through before grouping. Ownership of the through coach to Keith is less clear; the carriage working implies that it was a LMS vehicle. The remainder of the formation would almost certainly have contained LMS constituent company corridor vehicles, which had been drafted north, as well as Highland coaches. The Pullman car, which came off at Aviemore, in June 1927 was *Mauchline Belle*. It was one of three delivered to the LMS by the Clayton Wagon Company in 1923. A corridor coach on the Aberfeldy branch is notable for this time period. During July and August the train ran in two sections. The first departed at midday taking the Pullman car. At Aviemore the train was divided into two portions which travelled via Carr Bridge and Forres respectively. The second train departed Perth at 12.10 and travelled via Forres; a Restaurant Car was carried to Aviemore. The formations shown for 1938 are for this peak summer period. In fact three trains were run at this time, the third carrying two through coaches to Aviemore. New Restaurant Thirds were used on the first two trains, and the remainder of the stock in both probably consisted of LMS-built vehicles. Photographs taken in the early 1930s show Midland-built clerestory coaches leading the midday Pullman car train. Since the through coaches from Edinburgh were usually in this position, it is suggested that they were

Midland & North British Joint coaches which had been transferred to the LNER (Southern Scottish Area) in 1928.

Arrangements during the 1950s were slightly different. The train from Glasgow travelled via Carr Bridge and that from Edinburgh went via Forres. Portions from each were exchanged at Aviemore. BR standard coaches were employed for both trains by 1958, with an Unclassified Restaurant Car (possibly LNER) in the Edinburgh train. The LMS Restaurant Car added at Perth was working north to return on the up 'Royal Highlander'. Only the Glasgow train went to Inverness after 1963, the Edinburgh contribution being reduced to a portion added at Perth. This combined train was still in operation 10 years later but with less vehicles. A separate train from Edinburgh was reintroduced in the late 1970s. Vacuum-braked Mk 2 coaches began to appear in 1975 and mostly made up the sets until replaced by air-braked versions in the early 1980s.

Right:
An ex-Highland Railway Mail Van is the first vehicle in the 15.40 mail train to Perth leaving Inverness on 9 September 1950 in the charge of two Class 5 4-6-0s, No 45475 leading.
C. C. B. Herbert

Below:
The 06.40 Perth-Inverness leaving Aviemore in May 1960. Three coaches (C2, CC, BV) had been left at Aviemore to work to Inverness via Forres. The train is double-headed by Caledonian Pickersgill 4-4-0s Nos 54485 and 54486. *W. J. V. Anderson*

11.45 Ramsgate-Manchester/Liverpool (The 'Sunny South Express')

1926
Eastbourne dep 11.45

BC	BC	BC	B3	C3	RC	BC	B3	CC	C3	RC	BC

Corr Brake Composite — Eastbourne-Liverpool
Corr Brake Composite — Ramsgate-Liverpool
Corr Brake Composite — Ramsgate-Manchester
Corr Brake Third, Corr Third, Restaurant Composite 65ft, Corr Brake Composite — Eastbourne-Manchester
Corr Brake Third, Corr Composite, Corr Third — Eastbourne-Birmingham
Restaurant Composite 65ft, Corr Brake Composite — Ramsgate-Birmingham

Up working: Manchester dep 10.40

1934
Hastings dep 10.55

BC	B3	CC	O3	RC	CC	B3	C3	CC	B3

Corr Brake Composite (12/32) — Sheffield
Corr Brake Third (40), Corr Composite (18/32) — Liverpool
Open Third (56), Restaurant Composite 65ft, Corr Composite (18/32), Corr Brake Third (40) — Manchester
Corr Third (42), Corr Composite (18/32), Corr Brake Third (24) — Birmingham

Up working: Manchester dep 10.40

1939
Hastings dep 11.10

B3	CC	C3	CC	RC	B3	B3	CC	C3	BC

Corr Brake Third (24), Corr Composite (18/32) — Liverpool
Corr Third (56), Corr Composite (18/32), Restaurant Composite 65ft, Corr Brake Third (24) — Manchester
Corr Brake Third (24), Corr Composite (18/32), Corr Third (56) — Birmingham
Corr Brake Composite 60ft — Nottingham

Up working: Manchester dep 10.40

1981
Brighton dep 15.00

O2	O2	C1	BU	O2	O2	BV

Tourist Open Second
Tourist Open Second
Corr First
Miniature Buffet
Tourist Open Second
Tourist Open Second
Brake Van

BR Mk 1 stock
Up working: Manchester dep 07.27

1983
Brighton dep 13.49

O2	O2	O2	C1	O2	O2	O2	BV

Tourist Open Second
Tourist Open Second
Tourist Open Second
Corr First
Tourist Open Second Micro-Buffet
Tourist Open Second
Tourist Open Second
Brake Van

Mk 2 air-braked stock
Up working: Manchester dep 08.25 to Cardiff

This train was implemented in 1905 as a collaborative effort between the LNWR and the LBSCR. Departure was from Eastbourne with through coaches to Birmingham, Liverpool and Manchester with a Restaurant Car in the latter portion. Through coaches from Ramsgate were added after WW1. There were limited clearances on some of the Southern routes and the LNWR had built 8ft 6in-wide stock to accommodate such restrictions.

The formation shown for 1926 worked down on Tuesdays and Thursdays. On the other days a Southern Railway set was used but with LMS-owned Restaurant Cars. Coaches from the two southern resorts travelled separately to Willesden, via the West London Line, where they were combined and remarshalled. The Birmingham portion was dropped at Rugby, the remaining two portions being divided at Crewe. All the vehicles in the train at this time were 57ft types, apart from the Restaurant Cars.

Hastings soon became the starting point, instead of Eastbourne, as shown by the 1934 formation. A Brake Composite for Sheffield was detached from this 1934 set at Northampton; Bradford and Leeds had been destinations a few years earlier. However, the Ramsgate portion now only ran at weekends. Both sets were now supplied by the LMS, and modern stock had started to make an appearance.

The early summer weekend formation is shown for 1939. There were no major changes compared to five years earlier except that the through coach to the Midland line terminated at Nottingham.

With regard to the Restaurant Car employed, a 65ft LNWR diagram 358 Composite was specified until 1935. Following their withdrawal, WCJS diagram 9 composites with modified clearances were used.

The train did not reappear after WW2. It was not until 1979 that a Manchester-Brighton train was reintroduced. This time, the primary function was to serve Gatwick Airport rather than the holiday resorts as in prewar days. Mk 1 stock was used initially but this was replaced in 1982 by air-braked Mk 2 stock which was in turn supplanted by air-conditioned stock three years later.

Above:
A Birmingham (New St)-Hastings Restaurant Car Express consisting of LMS Period 3 and 'Porthole' stock crosses Southerham Bridge on the Brighton line, headed by LB&SCR Class I3 4-4-2T No 32076 on 22 July 1950. *S. C. Nash*

Secondary and Branch Line Formations

The LMS secondary and branch line carriage workings are illustrated here in two ways. First, the Western Division Carriage Working book issued in September 1933 is reviewed. Apparently after this date the information was published in a less permanent form, probably as duplicated sheets. This is the probable reason that information for subsequent years is difficult to obtain. Fortunately, Bill Rear of the Historical Model Railway Society has unearthed the Bangor station carriage workings for 1948. The author is indebted to him for permission to use some of this information for the second means of illustration.

According to the pamphlet *Information for the Guidance of Staff Dealing with Passenger-Carrying Vehicles etc* issued in June 1939, the types of non-corridor set in most general use on the Western Division were:

Inter-District set (three coaches)	**B3**	**C**	**B3**	
Lavatory set (four coaches)	**B3**	**C**	**C**	**B3**
Two-coach set	**C**	**B3**		

The 1933 Western Division Carriage working book contained over 1,000 items including strengthening coaches. There were three major groups of workings. The largest detailed 229 circuit workings for three-coach Inter-District sets which covered many of the secondary services south of Manchester and Liverpool. While the formation was not specified it would mainly have been Brake Third/Composite/Brake Third. Strengthening vehicles were often specified to be added for part of the daily circuit. A total of 78 four-coach Lavatory Sets were the next largest group. They were centred primarily in the North-West area and in North Wales. Their normal formation would have been two Composites flanked by a Brake Third at each end. However, a Third instead of a Composite, or a First and a Third substituted for two Composites, may also have been used. The next group contained 35 two-coach sets each consisting of a Composite and a Brake Third. They were based at several centres including Bletchley, Wolverhampton, Bolton and North Wales. Non-corridor 54ft LMS coaches would frequently have been used for all three groups, but as Jenkinson and Essery point out in *LMS Coaches*, older stock was often included with corridor vehicles becoming more prevalent during the 1930s. In addition, each district had its own allocation of sets for internal duties. Up to about 20 sets could be allocated to a district. Some of the branch line services covered by the district sets are given in Table 1. Again, little information was given regarding the class or type of vehicles used. Also included in Table 1 is a summary of the push-pull sets, (called 'motor trains' by the LMS), which operated in the Western Division. Most would have been made up of pre-grouping stock. A total of 165 LNWR coaches had been converted for motor train use either by the original owner or the LMS. Standard LMS non-corridor coaches were also converted for this purpose but there were only about 30 in 1933.

It is now necessary to go forward 15 years and consider the station working at Bangor. This is set out in Table 2 for the down local workings. Three-coach sets (3-sets), some with lavatory facilities (3-Lav Sets), were employed for most of the workings. Quite a few of them were strengthened with corridor or non-corridor coaches. Motor trains were used for some of the short-distance trips from Bangor.

Table 1: LMS Western Division — District Branch Line Services and Motor Trains, September 1933

		No of Sets
Abergavenny District	2-coach open set	9
Amlwch (inc Afonwen, Bethesda)	2-coach set	5
Ashbourne/Buxton	2-coach set	4
Blaenau Festiniog/ Llandudno Jct	2-coach set	5
Brecon/Hereford	4×6-wheel coach set	4
Brymbo/Mold	2-coach set	3
Carmarthen/Llandilo	2-coach set	2
Coalport/Wellington	3-coach set	2
Coniston and Lake Side	2-coach set	7
Denbigh/Rhyl	2-coach set	15
Penrith/Workington	3-coach set	6
Swansea/Pontardulais	2-coach set	3
	4-coach set	2
Swansea/Brynamman	4-coach set	11
Whitehaven/Carlisle	4-coach set (narrow stock)	7

Motor Trains:	
Amlwch	1
Bangor/Caernarvon/Llandudno	2
Bethesda	2
Bletchley/Bedford	1
Brynmawr/Ebbw Vale	1*
Burton/Tutbury	1
Northwich/Crewe	1
Denbigh/Mold/Rhyl	1
Dudley/Dudley Port	4
Holywell/Holywell Jct	1*
Leighton/Luton	1
Northampton/Blisworth	2
Oldham/Delph	1*
Over and Wharton/Warrington	1
St Albans/Watford	2
Seaton/Uppingham	2*
Stanmore	1*
Styal Line	1**
St Helens/Ditton/Warrington	8
Warwick/Blisworth/Northampton	1
Willesden/Clapham Jct/Victoria	1
Walsall/Wolverhampton	2
Newport Pagnell/Wolverton	1

*1-coach set: remainder 2-coach sets
**4-coach set

Above right:
Electrification brought Class 317 EMUs to the St Pancras/Moorgate-Bedford route. Unit No 307 leaves St Albans city on the 15.35 Luton-St Pancras working on 28 August 1983. *Paul D. Shannon*

Right:
A 2-coach set of Period 3 non-corridor coaches at Amlwch headed by Ivatt '2MT' 2-6-2T No 41323.
Real Photographs K2784

Table 2: Bangor Station Local Carriage Workings (Down) — Summer 1948

	Train	*Bangor dep*	*Formation*
	Bangor-Afonwen	04.51	3-Lav Set, 2×Corridor Composite
	Bangor-Amlwch	05.05	3-Set
	Bangor-Afonwen	05.45	3-Lav Set, 2×Third, Full Brake
	Bangor-Amlwch	06.35	3-Set
	Bangor-Caernarvon ECS	06.40	3-Set
	Bangor-Holyhead	07.30	3-Lav Set, Corridor Composite
07.45	Bethesda-Menai Bridge	08.10	Motor
05.45	Chester-Bangor	08.41*	3-Set, Corridor Third, Corridor Composite
06.10	Chester-Holyhead	09.12	3-Lav Set
08.42	Bethesda-Bangor	08.58*	Motor Train
	Bangor-Afonwen	09.00	3-Set
	Bangor-Caernarvon	09.35	3-Set, 2×Third
09.10	Llandudno Jct-Bangor	09.43*	3-Set, 3-Lav Set
07.40	Liverpool-Bangor	11.18*	3-Lav Set, 2×Thirds, 4×**
	Bangor-Caernarvon	11.25	3-Set, Corridor Third
09.20	Crewe-Holyhead	12.00	Corridor Brake Third, 2×Open Third, Corridor Composite, Corridor Brake Composite, Full Brake, Corridor Composite
11.50	Bethesda-Bangor	12.06*	Motor Train
11.35	Llandudno Jct-Bangor	12.10	3-Set
	Bangor-Afonwen	12.20	3-Lav Set, 2×Thirds
	Bangor-Amlwch	12.35	3-Lav Set
12.35	Bethesda-Bangor	13.28*	Motor Train
	Bangor-Holyhead	13.30	3-Lav Set, Corridor Third, Corridor Composite, Corridor Brake Composite
	Bangor-Caernarvon	13.40	Motor Train
12.35	Chester-Bangor	14.33*	3-Set, Corridor Composite, 4×**
	Bangor-Afonwen	14.45	3-Set, 2×Thirds
15.02	Llandudno-Holyhead	15.45	3-Lav Set, 3-Lav Set (detached)
	Bangor-Amlwch	15.55	3-Set
	Bangor-Afonwen	16.06	3-Lav Set, Corridor Brake Third
16.15	Llandudno Jct-Bangor	16.53*	3-Lav Set
16.45	Bethesda-Bangor	17.01*	Motor Train
	Bangor-Menai Bridge ECS	17.20	Motor Train
	Bangor-Amlwch	17.25	3-Set
	Bangor-Afonwen	17.30	3-Set
16.55	Llandudno Jct-Holyhead	17.45	3-Lav Set
17.55	Bethesda-Bangor	18.11*	Motor Train
17.42	Colwyn Bay-Bangor	18.23*	3-Lav Set
18.43	Llandudno Jct-Holyhead	19.30	3-Lav Set
	Bangor-Amlwch	19.45	3-Set
19.20	Llandudno Jct-Bangor	19.56*	3-Set, 2×Third
	Bangor-Afonwen	20.05	3-Set, 2×Third
20.10	Bethesda-Bangor	20.26*	Motor Train
17.05	Liverpool-Holyhead	20.40	Corridor Brake Third, Corridor Composite, Corridor Third, Corridor Brake Third
	Bangor-Caernarvon	20.52	3-Lav Set, Corridor Brake Third
19.20	Bethesda-Bangor	21.36*	Motor Train
21.18	Llandudno Jct-Bangor	21.51*	3-Lav Set
21.50	Llandudno Jct-Bangor	22.24*	3-Set
23.05	Llandudno Jct-Bangor	23.38*	3-Set

All coaches are non-corridor except where indicated

*Arrive
**Coaches determined by traffic office at Crewe

Appendices

1 — Extracts of General Notes from Carriage Working Books

LMS 1934

'Passenger trains must be made up strictly in accordance with the arrangements shown, and must not be altered without authority. Where brake carriages are next to the engine they must, as far as practicable, be run with the brake compartment in front.'

LM Region 1983

'Passenger trains must be made up strictly in accordance with the arrangements shown, and must not be altered without authority. A Brake Van or vehicle with brake compartment leading should, as far as practicable, be marshalled next to the engine except where the formation is otherwise specified . . . similarly a Brake Van or vehicle with brake compartment trailing, should, as far as practicable, be marshalled at the rear.

'In cases where two vehicles containing First Class accommodation, eg two Composite or Composite and Brake First, are scheduled to be marshalled together, the First Class sections of each coach should adjoin. Where two brake vehicles are scheduled to be marshalled together, the van ends should adjoin.

'On trains which convey a Dining or Refreshment Car, the following will apply except where otherwise shown:

'The Kitchen end of the Mk 1 Dining Car to be marshalled next to the Dining trailer vehicle (SO, FO etc).

'The Saloon end of the Mk 3 Dining Car (RUB) next to the Dining trailer vehicle (FO, TSO).

'The vehicle next to the Bar end to be marshalled with the lavatories adjacent to the Dining Car.'

2 — Drawing References for LMS and Absorbed Coaching Stock

The drawing references are from model railway magazines published from January 1950 to August 1986. The abbreviations used are:

MRC — *Model Railway Constructor*
RM — *Railway Modeller*
MRN — *Model Railway News* (published until August 1971)
MRY — *Model Railways* (published from September 1971): retitled *Your Model Railway* from October 1984

London Midland & Scottish Railway

Corridor Stock:

First (Diag 1747)	MRC	12/66
First (Diag 1748)	MRC	10/66
Composite (Diag 1694)	MRC	9/66
Composite (Diag 1716)	MRC	10/66
	RM	9/68
Composite (Diags 1925 & 2159)	RM	1/69
	RM	3/69
Third (Diag 1782)	MRC	12/67
Third (Diag 1899)	RM	7/66
Brake First (Diag 1654)	MRC	12/67
Brake First (Diag 1717)	MRC	12/67
	RM	9/68
Brake Composite (Diag 1720)	RM	7/68
Brake Composite (Diag 1755)	MRC	12/66
Brake Composite (Diags 1932 & 2010)	RM	3/69
Brake Third (Diag 1696)	MRC	9/66
	RM	11/68
Brake Third (Diag 1905)	RM	6/66

Vestibule Stock:

First (Diag 1707)	RM	11/67
First (Diag 1719)	MRC	12/67
Composite (Diag 1903)	RM	11/66
Third (Diag 1745)	MRC	1/66
Third (Diag 1807)	RM	5/68

Third (Diag 1904)	RM	9/66
First Brake Lounge (Diag 1741)	RM	11/67
Brake Third (Diag 1746)	MRC	1/66
12-wheel Composite Dining Car (Diag 1811)	RM	3/68
12-wheel Third Dining Car (Diags 1901 & 1923)	RM	1/68
12-wheel Composite Sleeping Car (Diag 1781)	RM	7/67
Non-corridor Stock:		
Composite (Diag 1701)	RM	1/67
Composite (Diag 1734)	RM	4/65
Third (Diag 1700)	RM	1/67
Third (Diag 1784)	RM	5/65
Brake Third (Diag 1703)	RM	3/67
Brake Third (Diag 1735)	RM	2/66
Push-Pull Brake Third (Diag 1790)	RM	11/64
	RM	7/85
Inter-district Set	MRC	10/65
Full Brake Van (Diag 1778)	MRC	4/65
	RM	5/67
6-wheel Full Brake Van	MRC	6/65
Parcels Van (Diag 1870)	RM	7/64
4-wheel Fish Van (Diag 1885)	RM	1/64
6-wheel Fish Van (Diag 2115)	RM	11/69
6-wheel Milk Van (Diag 1874)	RM	1/70
6-wheel Insulated Milk Van (Diag 1936)	RM	10/66
6-wheel Palethorpe's Sausage Van (Diag 1955)	RM	12/66
6-wheel Covered Combination Truck (Diag 1872)	RM	3/70
4-wheel Open Carriage Truck (Diag 2027)	MRC	8/61
4-wheel Horse Box (Diag 1956)	MRY	11/76

West Coast Joint Stock

50′ Arc Roof Corridor Stock:		
Composite (Diag 30)	MRC	9/71
Third (Diag 51)	MRC	9/71
Brake First (Diag 18)	MRC	9/71
Brake Composite (Diag 42)	MRC	9/71
Brake Third (Diag 67)	MRC	9/71
50′ Sleeping Saloon	MRC	9/72
68′ Sleeping Saloon (Diag W1)	MRY	8/86
42′ Travelling Post Office	MRC	7/70
64′ Travelling Post Office	MRC	9/72
6-wheel Parcels Sorting Van	MRC	12/68
6-wheel Fish Van (Diag 107)	MRY	6/73

Caledonian Railway

45′ Non-corr Composite	MRY	5/75
45′ Non-corr Third	MRY	5/75
57′ Corridor Composite	MRN	12/55
57′ Brake Composite	MRC	1/63
65′ 12-wheel 'Grampian' Stock	MRC	10/60
4-wheel Carriage Truck (Fish & Game Van)	MRY	1/75
6-wheel Carriage Truck	RM	11/59
Horse Box (1870)	RM	3/75

Furness Railway

4-wheel Early Carriage	RM	11/66
6-wheel 31′ Brake Third	RM	12/66
6-wheel Family Saloon	MRY	8/83
47′ Composite (Diag 21)	MRY	4/80
47′ Brake Composite (Diag 22)	MRY	2/80
48′ Third	MRC	3/63
	RM	12/66
Carriage Truck (1870)	MRY	2/81
Horse Box (1871)	MRY	8/80
Horse Box	RM	1/67

Garstang & Knott End Railway

Coach	MRN	10/59

Glasgow & South Western Railway

43′ First	RM	3/55
43′ Third	RM	3/55
6-wheel Post Office Sorting Van	MRN	8/56
6-wheel Full Brake	MRC	3/64
4-wheel Milk and Motor Car Van	MRY	7/75

Highland Railway

4-wheel Rib-sided Carriage	MRC	6/70
6-wheel Third (Diag 22)	MRC	12/81
Semi-corridor Composite	MRC	9/62
4-wheel Brake Van	RM	11/54
6-wheel Full Brake (Diag 38)	MRC	1/82
Full Brake	MRY	7/73
4-wheel Motor Car Van	RM	1/60
4-wheel Meat Van	MRC	5/67

Lancashire & Yorkshire Railway

Tri-composite (Diag 26A)	RM	9/78
Tri-composite (Diag 27A)	RM	9/78
Open Corridor Stock (1900):		
First	MRC	4/66
Third	MRC	4/66
Brake Composite	MRC	4/66
54′ Manchester-Oldham Stock:		
Composite	RM	7/78
Third	RM	7/78
Brake Third	RM	7/78
54′ Corridor Stock:		
Composite	MRC	7/61
Brake Composite	MRC	7/61
Fireproof Stock (1913):		
First	RM	1/79
Third	RM	1/79
Brake Third	RM	1/79
4-wheel Carriage Truck	RM	4/83
Covered Carriage Truck for Aeroplanes	MRY	2/73
4-wheel Milk Van	MRC	11/64
4-wheel Horse Box (Diag 108)	MRY	6/82
6-wheel Milk Van	MRC	11/64

London & North Western Railway

4-wheel Parliamentary (London & Birmingham Railway)	MRN	6/66
4-wheel Parliamentary (Manchester & Birmingham Railway)	MRC	9/68
6-wheel 30′ Stock:		
Tri-composite	MRC	1/69
Third	MRC	11/68
Brake Third	MRC	12/68
Full Brake	MRC	11/68
42′ First	MRC	7/70
42′ Tri-composite	MRC	6/70
50′ First	MRC	5/71
50′ Third	MRC	10/66
50′ Brake Third	MRC	5/71
50′ Arc Roof Corridor Stock:		
Composite	MRC	6/71

Third	MRC	6/71
Brake Third	MRC	6/71
Cove Roof Corridor Stock:		
57′ First	MRC	12/71
57′ Composite	MRC	12/71
57′ Third	MRC	12/71
57′ Brake Composite	MRC	12/71
50′ Brake Composite	MRC	12/71
57′ Corridor Stock:		
Composite	MRC	6/72
Third	MRC	6/72
Brake First	MRC	6/72
Brake Composite	MRC	6/72
Brake Third	MRC	6/72
Observation Car	MRC	1/83
Full Brake (Diag 380)	RM	7/85
Covered Scenery Truck (Diag 440)	MRY	4/73
Covered Scenery Truck (Diag 442)	MRY	5/73
6-wheel Parcels Van (Diag 385)	MRY	3/73
6-wheel Milk Brake Van	MRY	2/73
6-wheel Fruit Van (Diag 454)	MRY	5/74
	MRY	8/82
6-wheel Fish Van	MRY	6/73
4-wheel Combination Truck (Diag 444)	MRY	8/72
4-wheel Combination Truck (Diag 444A)	MRY	7/72
4-wheel Combination Truck (Diag 445)	MRY	12/72
	MRY	8/82
4-wheel Combination Truck (Diag 445A)	MRY	1/73
	MRY	8/82
4-wheel Covered Truck for Motor Car (Diag 446)	MRY	9/72
4-wheel Motor Car Truck (Diag 448)	MRY	11/74
4-wheel Covered Truck for HM Motor Car	MRY	11/72
4-wheel Chassis Non-passenger Stock	MRN	6/62
6-wheel Chassis Non-passenger Stock	MRN	6/62

Maryport & Carlisle Railway

6-wheel Composite (1890)	MRY	4/81
6-wheel 31′ Third (Diag 8)	MRY	4/80
6-wheel Third	MRN	1/67
4-wheel Brake	MRN	1/67
Horse Box	MRY	2/74

Midland Railway

4-wheel Parliamentary	MRN	2/66
6-wheel 31′ Composite	MRN	3/60
54′ Corridor, Clerestory Roof Stock:		
First	MRC	9/58
Composite	MRC	4/68
Third	MRC	6/68
Brake Composite	MRC	5/68
Brake Third	MRC	4/68
	MRC	6/55
Slip Brake Composite	MRC	11/55
Chassis and 8′ Bogie	MRC	5/68
Open Third, Clerestory Roof	MRC	10/64
Railmotor No 2234	MRC	10/74
	MRC	11/74
Railmotor Trailer No 2235	MRC	10/74
	MRC	11/74
Pullman Cars (1874)	MRN	1/59
6-wheel Clerestory Full Brake Van	MRN	4/56
6-wheel 31′ Full Brake Van	MRY	6/74
6-wheel Parcels Van	MRY	8/75
6-wheel Motor Car Van	MRY	6/75
4-wheel 25′ Milk Van	MRY	11/73
4-wheel Covered Carriage Truck (Diag 402)	MRY	9/73
4-wheel Covered Carriage Truck (Diag 403)	MRY	8/73
4-wheel Covered Carriage Truck (Diag 406)	MRY	10/73
Horse Boxes (Various Diags)	MRY	4/7

North London Railway

4-wheel Coaches	RM	12/71
4-wheel Full Brake	RM	12/71

North Staffordshire Railway

49′ Brake Third	MRC	7/62
Inspection Saloon No 356	MRY	1/75
Inspection Saloon — Petrol	MRY	4/75
4-wheel Milk Van	MRY	1/74
6-wheel Milk Van	MRY	1/74

Somerset & Dorset Joint Railway

4-wheel First Nos 1-4	MRY	6/76
4-wheel First No 5	MRY	12/76
4-wheel Composite (Long Wheelbase)	MRY	8/77
4-wheel Third	MRY	3/76
4-wheel Third (Long Wheelbase)	MRY	8/77
4-wheel Brake Third	MRY	7/76
4-wheel Full Brake	MRY	8/77
4-wheel Close Coupled Stock:		
Second	MRY	7/77
Third	MRY	7/77
Brake Third	MRY	7/77
6-wheel 28′ 5″ Composite	MRY	5/78
6-wheel 31′ Stock:		
First	MRY	9/78
Composite	MRY	5/78
	MRC	7/75
Third	MRY	9/78
	MRC	7/75
Brake Third	MRY	12/79
	MRY	5/80
Underframe	MRY	9/78
46′ Composite	MRY	12/85
	MRY	7/80
46′ Composite Luggage	MRY	7/80
46′ Third	MRY	6/84
46′ Brake Third	MRY	11/83
4-wheel Milk Van	MRY	10/73
4-wheel 25′ Fruit Van	MRY	11/73
6-wheel 30′ Full Brake	MRY	12/79
	MRC	7/75
32′ Underframe	MRY	12/79

In addition, the following books contain a significant number of drawings:

LMS Coaches, D. Jenkinson and R. J. Essery (Oxford Publishing Company).
An Illustrated History of LNWR Coaches (Including West Coast Joint Stock), D. Jenkinson (Oxford Publishing Company).
Midland Railway Carriages (Vols 1 and 2), R. E. Lacy and George Dow (Wild Swan).
Midland Carriages, David Jenkinson and R. J. Essery (Oxford Publishing Company).